IN ORDER TO

We must first make an artful life, a life rich enough and diverse enough to give us fuel. We must strive to see the beauty where we are planted, even if we are planted somewhere that feels very foreign to our own nature. In New York, I must work to connect to the parts of the city that feed my imagination and bring me a sense of richness and diversity instead of mere overcrowding and sameness. In California, my friend must work to do the same. We must, as the elders advise us, bloom where we are planted. If we later decide that we must be transplanted, that our roots are not in soil rich enough for our spirits, at least we have tried. We have kept hold of the essential thread of our consciousness, the "I" that gives us the eye to behold.

—from THE SOUND OF PAPER

THE SOUND OF PAPER

NONFICTION

The Artist's Way

The Artist's Way Morning Pages Journal

The Artist's Date Book
  (illustrated by Elizabeth Cameron)

Walking in This World

The Vein of Gold

The Right to Write

God Is No Laughing Matter

Prayers from a Nonbeliever

Supplies

God Is Dog Spelled Backwards
  (illustrated by Elizabeth Cameron)

Heartsteps

Blessings

Transitions

Inspirations: Meditations from *The Artist's Way*

The Writer's Life: Insights from *The Right to Write*

The Artist's Way at Work
  (with Mark Bryan and Catherine Allen)

Money Drunk, Money Sober *(with Mark Bryan)*

FICTION

Popcorn: Hollywood Stories

The Dark Room

JEREMY P. TARCHER/PENGUIN

a member of Penguin Group (USA) Inc.

New York

The
Sound
of
Paper

STARTING

FROM SCRATCH

Julia
Cameron

JEREMY P. TARCHER/PENGUIN
Published by the Penguin Group
www.penguin.com
Penguin Group (USA) Inc., 375 Hudson Street, New York, New York 10014, USA • Penguin Group
(Canada), 10 Alcorn Avenue, Toronto, Ontario, Canada M4V 3B2 (a division of Pearson Penguin
Canada Inc.) • Penguin Books Ltd, 80 Strand, London WC2R 0RL, England • Penguin Ireland,
25 St Stephen's Green, Dublin 2, Ireland (a division of Penguin Books Ltd) • Penguin Group
(Australia), 250 Camberwell Road, Camberwell, Victoria 3124, Australia (a division of Pearson
Australia Group Pty Ltd) • Penguin Books India Pvt Ltd, 11 Community Centre, Panchsheel Park,
New Delhi–110 017, India • Penguin Group (NZ), Cnr Airborne and Rosedale Roads, Albany,
Auckland, New Zealand (a division of Pearson New Zealand Ltd) • Penguin Books (South Africa)
(Pty) Ltd, 24 Sturdee Avenue, Rosebank Johannesburg 2196, South Africa

Penguin Books Ltd, Registered Offices: 80 Strand, London WC2R 0RL, England

First trade paperback edition 2005
Copyright © 2004 by Julia Cameron

Most Tarcher/Penguin books are available at special quantity discounts for bulk purchase for sales
promotions, premiums, fund-raising, and educational needs. Special books or book excerpts also can
be created to fit specific needs. For details, write Penguin Group (USA) Inc. Special Markets, 375
Hudson Street, New York, NY 10014.

Library of Congress cataloged the hardcover edition as follows:
Cameron, Julia.
The sound of paper : starting from scratch / Julia Cameron.
p. cm.
ISBN 1-58542-288-6
1. Creation (Literary, artistic, etc.). 2. Self-actualization (Psychology). I. Title.
BF408.C1758 2004 2003061411
153.3'5—dc22
ISBN 1-58542-354-8 (paperback edition)

Printed in the United States of America
1 3 5 7 9 10 8 6 4 2

This book is printed on acid-free paper. ∞

Book design by Marysarah Quinn

This book is dedicated to Joel Fotinos,
who has taught me to approach
the changing seasons of my life with faith.

ACKNOWLEDGMENTS

Sophy Burnham, for her creative courage
Elizabeth Cameron, for her loyalty
Domenica Cameron-Scorsese, for her artful heart
Sara Carder, for her meticulousness
Carolina Casperson, for her belief
Sonia Choquette, for her believing mirror
James Dybas, for his generosity
Joel Fotinos, for his faith
Candice Fuhrman, for her support
Natalie Goldberg, for her example
Kelly Groves, for his enthusiasm
H.O.F., for his artistry
Linda Kahn, for her clarity
Bill Lavallee, for his service
Emma Lively, for her catalytic collaboration
Larry Lonergan, for his vision
Julianna McCarthy, for her creativity
John Newland, for his lessons
Bruce Pomahac, for his friendship
Johanna Tani, for her care
Jeremy Tarcher, for his leadership
Edmund Towle, for his perspective

THE SOUND OF PAPER

INTRODUCTION

The small book you hold in your hands was begun in a green eastern spring and written throughout a long, parched summer in New Mexico. It is intended as a creative companion. Its essays are modest and gentle. Each is accompanied by a matching task, also modest and gentle. It is my belief that we make great strides in our creativity by taking little steps. Think of this book as a summer's hike through the New Mexico wilderness. You will gradually build stamina and savvy. One essay at a time, one task at a time, you will become more and more familiar with your own creative strengths.

IN YOUR BACKPACK

There are three creative tools that should be undertaken and continued throughout your work with this book—and, I hope, far beyond.

MORNING PAGES: Morning Pages are the pivotal tool of a successful creative life. They are three pages of longhand, morning writing, about anything and everything. You may complain, whine, grumble, grieve. You may hope, celebrate, plan, plot. Nothing is too small or too large to be included. Everything is grist for the creative mill. Why should we do Morning Pages? Morning Pages prioritize our day. They render us present to the moment. They introduce us to an unsuspected inner strength and agility. They draw to our attention those areas of our life that need our focus. Both our weaknesses and our strengths will be gently revealed. Problems will be exposed, and solutions suggested.

Morning Pages are a potent form of meditation for hyperactive Westerners. They amplify what spiritual seekers call "the still small voice." Work with the Morning Pages awakens our intuition. Synchronicity becomes a daily fact. We are more and more often in the right place at the right time. We know how to handle situations that once baffled us. In a very real sense, we become our own friend and witness. Morning Pages are the gateway to the inner and higher self. They bring us guidance and resilience. They make us farseeing. I have been doing Morning Pages for two decades now. Many of my students have used them a decade or longer. They are a portable, reliable, and friendly tool. Do Morning Pages daily.

ARTIST DATES: The Artist Date is the companion tool to Morning Pages. It is a once-a-week, festive outing undertaken and executed solo. As the name suggests, the tool involves self-romancing. On an Artist Date, we become intimate with ourselves, our hopes, dreams, and aspirations. Many students report that it was on an Artist Date that they first felt conscious contact with the Great Creator. An Artist Date *is* sacred time. It is time set aside to nurture our creative consciousness. In planning an Artist Date, think mystery rather than mastery. Think pleasure, not duty. Choose an expedition that enchants you, one that truly interests your inner explorer. In planning and executing Artist Dates, expect to encounter a certain amount of inner resistance. Despite seeming frivolous, the Artist Date is a serious tool for self-discovery. Commit yourself to overcoming your resistance. Take one Artist Date weekly.

WALKS: The third pivotal creative tool is one that links together mind and body. This tool is walking. Like the Morning Pages and the Artist Date, it is deceptively simple, yet very powerful. A twenty-minute Walk is long enough. An additional hour's Walk once weekly is recommended. What does walking do? It nudges us out of our habitual thinking. It builds a bridge to higher consciousness. It allows us to access our intuition, to focus on solutions rather than problems. Try for two to three short Walks weekly, and one long one.

Setting Off

IT IS A BRIGHT AND CHILL early spring day. The air is crisp but the earth is insistent. In Riverside Park, jonquils are in bloom wherever they are sheltered. On a slight and unshaded hill, purple crocuses push past frosty grass. Small bushes sprout tiny buds, some green-gold, some reddish-brown. The distant trees are misted by the lightest tincture of green, like a delicate Japanese watercolor. The wind is stiff and needling. It still feels like winter, but spring itself is positive and determined. Something is afoot, and it is festive and uncontrollable and undeniable. "Just wait and see," it says, but who wants to wait? Spring invites and invokes curiosity. Mine has been as insistent and pushy as the not-to-be-denied buds.

This afternoon, scratching this itch, I took an Artist Date. I went to the Museum of Natural History and walked through an exhibit on pearls. My fellow viewers were as interesting as any of the glassed-in exhibits. There were fine old ladies, alert as tiny songbirds. There were sturdy, bespectacled teacherly types peering owlishly at the fine print. There were misplaced shoppers, strutting like peacocks, fingering their gaudy modern clothes and gazing at the past century's finery. And there I was in the middle of them, a pale, wild-haired woman sporting real pearl earrings and wincing at the documentary that showed in gory detail exactly how cultured pearls are induced and harvested.

As is often the case when I stick my nose into things, I learned more than I bargained for. I do not live well with excruciating detail. What I am after is "enough"—enough to set the writing gears going, which may not be very much. Sometimes just a pinch of information is enough. A case in point: Today I learned, in my learning about pearls, that pearls are what happen when an oyster or some other mollusk is irritated by the invasion of some disturbing intruder into its closed shell. An infinitesimal shrimp may get caught in an oyster and become the tiny intruder around which a pearl is built. A grain of sand may be slight but not too slight to cause a pearl to form. Pearls are layers and layers of soothing "nacre" intended to insulate the delicate mollusk from the irritant that has abraded it. At root, a pearl is a "disturbance," a beauty caused by something that isn't supposed to be there, about which something needs to be done. It is the interruption of equilibrium that creates beauty. Beauty is a response to provocation, to intrusion. "How like art," I catch myself thinking. The pearl's beauty is made as a result of insult just as art is made as a response to something in our environment that fires us up, sparks us, causes us to think differently. The pearl, like art, must be catalyzed. And we, unlike the mollusk, can invite the disturbance that provokes us into art.

Lately, I am trying to provoke myself into art—at the least I am trying to provoke myself into writing. I spent a hard winter writing and rewriting a difficult book. That book, which may have turned out well after all, left me feeling stale and flat. I doubted I would ever have another book in me. I thought after thirty-five years of writing that maybe it was time to stop, that just maybe I had written enough—and a little more than enough by at least a book's worth. I wasn't exactly in despair—that would have taken too much energy. I was in cynicism, which is despair's more torpid sister.

Cynicism lacks any real conviction. It doesn't like the game as it's being played, and so it spoils it. At bottom, cynicism is a cheap and shoddy response to a life we are afraid to love because it might, for a time, be painful. My writing life, for a time, had proved painful, and so I wanted a way to wriggle out of it and have some other life, exactly what, I wasn't sure. Let me tell you how writing snuck back in on me.

First of all, I write daily. I do three pages of longhand morning writing, whether I am writing my "real" writing or not. The pages are not what I think of as writing. They are more my wake-up call, the pen-to-page that sends me into my day, with that day somewhat prioritized or at least freed from the gripes of yesterday. So, the three pages began sliding toward four pages and then toward five. This happened with disturbing regularity, and it happened because I wasn't writing—except those three pages. Next I began binge reading, another way to cozy up to words. I whipped through a half dozen books and found myself browsing on the Internet for excuses to order more. Before I knew it, I had spent three hundred dollars on books. I waited for their arrival—"same-day delivery" here in Manhattan—like a ravenous dog. No, I wasn't writing and I wasn't going to write. I was just going to nose around a little and see what my other writer friends were up to, see if any of them still liked writing. One of them had told me not a month earlier that she had sworn off. Was she still on the wagon, I wondered, or had words started to have their way with her again? Was she staggering to the page punch-drunk with a need to say something, anything? Nothing gets a writer more off center than not writing, and she had certainly sounded crabby about her high-minded decision to "just be a person."

The truth is that writing cannot really be given up any more than acting or music can. All that happens when you give up an art that you love—although you may hate it at the moment—is that you get one of those divorces where you are much too curious about your ex's love life. And so, while I toyed with the idea of never writing again or writing only music, I also knew enough to recognize that I already had the symptoms of recovery. There were the tell-tale extra pages tacked onto my Morning Pages. There were the stacks of books—all filled with words, glorious words—piling up next to my bed like a delicious mound of mental lingerie. There were those snoopy calls to other writers to see how they were doing with swearing off their affliction. Do I need to tell you that my on-the-wagon friend was writing again, "just a little"?

Have you guessed that I am writing just a little too? I am, I am, and my excursions are intended to help me spill words onto the page a little more easily and happily. I have learned that if I take my artist on a date, it responds like any other sullen romantic interest. After a while, it stops sulking and it talks to me. It has ideas to share and so, like spatting lovers meeting "just for a moment," it shares a coquettish thought—just to get me interested. It asks a question that sets me to thinking, and soon, there we are, at it again.

It has occurred to me that a book of questions is a conversation that I could enjoy having right now. I can feel myself being coaxed out of hiding and into a real dialogue. There are a great many questions I am often asked about creativity, and I have many ideas about how exactly they should be answered. Hence this book: a creative troubleshooting guide for those who have been put off their creativity.

SETTING OFF

Try this: Gather fifteen or twenty magazines with pictures. Purchase a large piece of poster board and some glue. Supply yourself with scissors and some tape. Set aside one hour. For the first half hour, pull images that speak to you from the magazines. You do not need to know why you connect to a certain image; it is enough that you do. For the second half hour, trim and paste your images onto the poster board. You are making a portrait of your consciousness at this point in time. What you see in your collage may surprise, delight, or even alarm you. Seeing *is* believing, and one picture is worth a thousand words. Using words, take to the page and describe your personal discoveries.

❧

Who, Me?

TONIGHT I AM GOING to a dinner party—a Manhattan dinner party, black dress optional, but perhaps expected. As a child, I read *Vogue* magazine and plotted to live in New York. New York, I thought, was where the grown-ups live. I still think that.

Twelve years old, lying on the floor by the heating vent in the front hallway, underneath the curving banister that led upstairs. Supermodels were a new phenomenon—Verushka, Lauren Hutton, photo spreads in Africa with Peter Beard. Just Verushka and a stray lion, gazelle, hippopotamus. Nothing she wore could actually be worn, certainly not by a twelve-year-old or even by the adult that twelve-year-old might grow into, but what fun it was to look. Verushka painted blue like some wild African tribesman. Verushka, sleek as a panther, inclining herself on some low-lying bough.

I don't know how many New Yorkers grew up somewhere else, dreaming of New York, but I did. I studied layouts of Chanel suits and Dior. I learned hemlines and hairstyles, the color of this year's acceptable nail lacquer and lipstick. I weighed tote bags and sunglasses, sandals and belts: the "right" accessories.

New York meant much more than New York. It meant sophistication, taste, freedom, and accomplishment. It meant you had "made it" somehow, creatively, and that your life, a New Yorker's life, was chief among your creations. New Yorkers read *The New Yorker* and strolled through its pages in a William Hamilton car-

toon. New Yorkers wrote for *The Village Voice* and answered dar-
ing personal ads placed by daring city dwellers like themselves.
New Yorkers were literate and stylish and up-to-the-minute.
They had savoir faire, and knew what to wear and how to wear it.
For an adult New Yorker, a dinner party like tonight's was a snap.
"Why, I'll just wear my black suit and my spangled black cardigan
with the tiny jet beads."

Somehow, although I have lived in New York off and on now
for twenty years, I have never quite made it to "a New Yorker."
Dinner parties like tonight's, at the home of a chic *Gourmet* editor, leave me wondering, "The black suit or the navy blue?
Clearly an evening out, or a continuation of a busy day's look?"
New Yorkers themselves strike me mute. They have country
houses and manage to juggle rents and mortgages with a sleight
of hand that still leaves me feeling uneasy.

Of course, the magazines are still full of advice on how they
manage it. New York is still the epicenter of the magazine publishing world, and try as they may to include Des Moines's reader-
ship in their far-flung net, it is still New York and New Yorkers
that we read about. "Managing to swing that country house" is
not a topic that a Des Moines reader needs to bone up on—but I
still do. Curled in my reading chair, looking out at my New York
view, I still read articles on how to be chic—New York–style—
with the same baffled avidity I did as a precocious child.

Tonight's dinner party will feature live and in-the-flesh New
York writers. I am one of them now.

WHO, ME?

Try this: Each of us has a different idea of sophistication. Each of us has certain items that speak to us as tokens of success. Sometimes in all our striving, we overlook treating ourselves symbolically in ways that match our accomplishments. Take pen in hand and number from 1 to 25. List twenty-five things that represent to you sophistication and success. For example:

1. *Red nail polish*
2. *A good writing implement*
3. *Handsome business cards*
4. *Enough socks*
5. *Leather gloves*

Scanning over your list, select a symbolic something by which you can celebrate your soigné adulthood.

The Life of
the Imagination

IT IS A GRAY, dreary, and socked-in day, more like February than May. I am living in New York, on the farthest-west street in the city, right on the Hudson, but today is a day without bearings as the fog mists over the river and the Jersey shore beyond. It erases, too, nearby buildings and makes all of consciousness just this window into never-never land. I sit at this typewriter, tapping keys like Morse code across the murky landscape sending messages to . . . somewhere.

This morning I talked with a good friend of mine, also a writer. She has washed up in California, not feeling at home with where she finds herself, in a tiny apartment in Silicon Valley, marooned on a seedbed of high finance, far from her beloved New Mexico with its endless vistas and gentle optimism bred in the beauty of the land. She hates Silicon Valley, hates the fact that she is unhappy and scared: "It has come to this?" I know how she feels. Her whole life shrunk to the size of the room where she is penned in and trying to put words to the page.

For me, living in New York is a tricky balancing act. Daily, I must leave the cage of my apartment and venture out into the city. Then I must get in, out of the city, back to my apartment nest. The cage/nest contradiction is a constant one. It goes with the urban terrain. The enchantment of New York is its big dreams. The reality of New York is its small living spaces.

Today I went to briefly visit the town house of a garden designer, a good friend of a good friend. She lives on the ground floor of a brownstone that she owns. Her apartment, with its greenhouse addition at the rear and her garden beyond, has a wildness and beauty to it uncommon in New York. But her floor-through itself is small and dark. Her bedroom fronts onto a crosstown street and her bed is mere feet away from traffic. By being on the ground floor, she gains her garden, but she gains street noise as well—and a view of passing feet. I have always chosen to live high up, looking out over the park or the city from a bird's-eye view, anything not to feel trapped and run to earth. She has chosen to live on the earth, plunging her hands into a patch of dirt so that she knows she owns something, some green spot in all the brick and concrete.

As an artist, so much of my life is determined by the size of my imagination. If I am making something big, and making it daily, I can perhaps live somewhere small. I can sit at a desk that faces a wall and tap words into space and my world is still large enough. When I write my opera about Magellan, in some sense I am Magellan. I am more than my circumstances, more than the cage of my environment. There is a dignity inherent in making art, a filament of largesse and generosity, a connection to something better and brighter than myself. Like the concentration camp victim who scratched butterflies into the walls of his prison, I see that the primacy of the flight of imagination is the freedom that is required. "You do not own me," I am able to say to the walls that enclose me. And yet, I must learn to love my walls.

My friend who is living in California is not really living there. She is doing time, living out her sentence until she can escape again. She has done what I have often and dangerously done—cut herself off from making new connections and friends, made a judgment, and lived miserably within its confines. "These people are not my kind," she has decided, and so she is isolated, a foreigner living amid foreign customs and mores. She may be right about that, but, right or wrong, the decision cuts her off and robs her even of that cherished writer's niche, the observer. If she is too closed down to even risk the exposure of watching, then she is losing the terrain that gives her a writing life in the future: "The years I lived in California . . ."

It is difficult to commit to living where we are, how we are. It is difficult and it is necessary. In order to make art, we must first make an artful life, a life rich enough and diverse enough to give us fuel. We must strive to see the beauty in where we are planted, even if we are planted somewhere that feels very foreign to our own nature. In New York, I must work to connect to the parts of the city that feed my imagination and bring me a sense of richness and diversity instead of mere overcrowding and sameness. In California, my friend must work to do the same. If we are not willing to work in this way, we become victims. If we become victims, we first become choiceless and then become voiceless. Our art dries up at the root. We must, as the elders advise us, bloom where we are planted. If we later decide that we must be transplanted, that our roots are not in soil rich enough for our spirits, at least we have tried. We have kept hold of the essential thread of our consciousness, the "I" that gives us the eye to behold.

THE LIFE OF THE
IMAGINATION

Try this: It takes practice to expand our imagination and inhabit a larger life. Certain phrases
can stretch our imagination in positive directions. Take pen in hand and explore one such
phrase now. Number from 1 to 10, and finish
the following phrase as rapidly as possible. Do
use the "best" in "the best of all possible worlds."

1. *If the best of all possible worlds were reality,
    I would have a sunny, spacious New York
    apartment with views.*
2. *If the best of all possible worlds were reality,
    my plays would be produced in great venues.*
3. *If the best of all possible worlds were reality,
    I would be thin and fit, running daily.*
4. *If the best of all possible worlds were reality,*

_____.

5. *If the best of all possible worlds were reality,*

   _____.

6. *If the best of all possible worlds were reality,*

   _____.

7. *If the best of all possible worlds were reality,*

   _____.

8. *If the best of all possible worlds were reality,*

   _____.

9. *If the best of all possible worlds were reality,*

   _____.

10. *If the best of all possible worlds were reality,*

   _____.

If the best of all possible worlds were reality, most of us would do things a little differently. We can begin to make the best a reality by doing things a little differently now.

Point Zero

WHEN WE ARE AT ZERO, we have to start somewhere, and perhaps the sanest, best, and surest place to start is with the eye of the beholder. We are in a certain place at a certain time and we feel a certain way about it. Let's start here. That means put the pen to the page and write about the exact moment and place where you find yourself. Take an inventory of what surrounds you and what you feel about that. This is a starting-off place.

I am writing in a wedge-shaped yellow room that looks west across the Hudson River toward America. The yellow of the room is a golden yellow, the color of sunflowers and golden hope. The furniture in this room is rich and substantial: a leather couch and reading chair, a "good" piano, Oriental cabinets and chests and rugs, handsome and well-framed Audubon prints, some well-mounted vintage photographs of Rodgers and Hammerstein. Everything bespeaks permanency and solidity. It is lying. I have this room a few scant months more, and then I will need to find another Manhattan perch, hopefully one that will be better and sunnier than this one, perhaps one with city views that will speak to me of the large community I am a part of. Looking at this room, taking in my feelings about it, I see that I am not nowhere, I am somewhere uncomfortable. This is what writing teaches us. Where we are really. Where we are is often the first clue to who we are.

It takes courage to put ourselves out on the page, but it is better to be in reality than in denial. Reality is a place to start something. Denial is a place where something is already going on that we do not want to see and be a part of even though we are. When most of us say we are zeroed out, we are in fact someplace we can start from, not nowhere at all. The trick, the first trick, lies in admitting exactly where we are.

My friend who is marooned in California is in a place she feels alien to, and that is a place that is relative to other places where she has lived and been more comfortable and more comforted. In other words, her history is a place to stand on, a strand of continuity that can be picked up and examined. She can say, "I liked the Midwest and the Southwest." She is not merely adrift, saying, "I don't like this." She is saying, or able to say, "I don't like this as compared to that." She has not only the place she is now but another place that she can or cannot get back to and that held values that are clues to the values she is missing now.

We do not arrive willy-nilly at point zero. We arrive there a choice at a time, a degree at a time, as we make little or less than we should of a growing discomfort. We get along without what we love the way camels get along without water—not forever, but for a very long time. And then, one day, we are thirsty and what we crave is water, real water, a pure infusion of something that matches what our body and soul are authentically craving.

When we are at point zero, and in despair, we are at the point of experiment. We must pick ourselves up somehow and we must make ourselves feel better and more comfortable. How can we do that? What do we need? Do we need a phone call to a friend? Do we need to get out of town altogether and go for a good, long drive? Something will speak to us of the good mother giving us what we crave, and we must listen to that craving and try to act on it. We must gentle our restless heart by saying and meaning, "I am listening to you. I hear your discomfort. I will work with you to change it."

Putting a pen to the page is the beginning of communication. We are writing a letter to our self. We are saying, "This is what I like and this is what I dislike." We are saying, "This is what I hope for." Or "This is what I dream of." We are saying, "This is what I am smack-dab in the middle of, and I do not like it."

Such communication is vital, and it is what we often neglect. Instead of putting our specific lives into black and white where we can see them and do something about them, we leave them vague, unspoken, and unwritten. "Something" is bothering us, but we don't know what it is. We sweep our feelings under the carpet. We turn a deaf ear to our quiet desperation. We are not ready or willing to attend to ourselves, and our souls know this. They are alert to the fact that they are ignored and unhusbanded. Is it any wonder that they are depressed?

And so, the first act of loving kindness is to start from scratch—the scratch of a pen to paper. The filling of blank pages with our specific likes and dislikes, our heartfelt and regretted losses and sacrifices—this is the beginning of being someone and some-where again. When we ignore ourselves for too long, we become exhausted and weakened from trying to get our own attention. We become disheartened—without a heart. The gentle pulse that we are meant to attend to, the ear-cocked, mothering side of our-selves that listens to a newborn and springs into action on its behalf, must be mustered now to come to our own rescue. But the rescue begins with the act of writing. Writing is how we "right" our world.

My friend in California does not like the expense of where she is living, where every inch of space has a price tag on it that strikes her as too high. "Imagine, paying two thousand dollars for a one-bedroom apartment," she snorts. She has the money but she resents spending it. She feels she is buying herself a gilded and glorified cage. Back where she likes it, that same two thousand dollars might rent a palatial house or easily cover a mortgage payment. There is something about spending money on a place she doesn't like that strikes her as wasteful and wrong. She is not spending money for something she cherishes. She is spending money for something for which she has contempt. "This place. There are no real buildings like back in Saint Paul. It is all malls."

A page at a time, a line at a time, we draw the outline of what it is that is paining us. My friend misses the four-square architecture of the Midwest, the honesty she felt in redbrick buildings that would stand up even if the wind huffed and puffed. "The buildings out here are terrible," she wails, talking about the prefab, jerry-rigged, tossed-up lightweight "buildings" that she encounters daily in California. The very building materials strike her as shoddy—as nothing that she can endorse. Now she is getting somewhere. Isn't what is bothering her the idea that she is somehow cosigning a lifestyle that she does not feel is in deep harmony with her own? There is very little wrong with California per se; it is the strike-it-rich pipe dream of Silicon Valley that she is objecting to. The American dream with dollars crunched in its talons.

My friend continued. "I went to dinner with some people the other night and they were nice enough, but afterward, I said to my partner, 'What do they do?' and my partner said, 'They enjoy their lives.'" She wondered, "Aren't we supposed to do something more than enjoy our lives, aren't we supposed to have made a difference in our passage here?" Now my friend is getting down to brass tacks, getting down to what is really bothering her: a life with no purpose. That is why she feels unmoored in Silicon Valley. She cannot relate to a life where the primary purpose is the making of money and the purchasing of creature comforts. Now that she knows what is bothering her about "them," she can start to ask about herself.

What would give her life a sense of purpose and connection? What commitment can she make to deeper values so that she does not feel that her values are adrift?

When we are building a life from scratch, we must dig a little. We must be like that hen scratching the soil: What goodness is hidden here, just below the surface? We must ask. We ask that question by putting pen to page.

POINT ZERO

Try this: Take a blank sheet of paper. Draw a circle and divide that circle into six wedges. Label the wedges as follows: work, recreation, spirituality, friendship, adventure, physicality. Place a dot in each a wedge indicating your satisfaction in that area. The closer to the outer rim you place the dot, the more satisfied you are. Now connect the dots. Does your life resemble a hexagon of even satisfaction? Or a tarantula of frustration? Choose any area in which you do not have optimum satisfaction. Number from 1 to 10 and list ten small changes you *could* make in that area.

Attention

I HAVE BEEN WRITING this little book for just over a month. In the time that I have been writing, the spring trees have filled out to a bouffant fullness. The winter's black, line-drawing limbs are covered with fluff. My view of the river is blocked now by my view of the trees. It is almost time to get in the car and drive with the dogs cross-country, out to Taos, where the views stretch a hundred miles across great green sage-clothed plains to purple mountains.

I am eager to make the drive, eager to be where I can see distance again and eager, too, to look at New York from a distance, to see how it feels to look back here from out there. In other words, I am eager to connect the dots, to fill in the puzzle pieces, to keep writing. Every book I undertake is a journey, and it is a journey made from specific point to specific point. For each of us, each and every day is also a journey. A journey that begins with us at a certain point, feeling a certain way, and ends with us being somewhere different and feeling how we feel about that. This is why there is never really a zero point to be at.

"Oh, who cares," we sometimes think at our most blue moments. "I am boring and it is boring and writing about it all is boring too." At times like these we need to imagine that we are writing to someone who listens to us with the rapt attention of a new lover. Someone who wants to discover all there is to know about us, all we think, all we have thought, even all we might soon think. I believe that there is such a lover with an ear cocked to all of us. That lover, that loving attention, is the Great Creator, who does not find us dull but endlessly interesting.

Attention is an act of connection. We look from where we are to what is all around us. In doing so, we discover where we are at. The "I" that connects becomes the "eye of the beholder." We see something, we notice it, we feel this way or that about it. When we feel we are at zero, we are never at zero. We are at the point of connection, the tiny vanishing point of consciousness where the "I" is born. We are, perhaps, the tiny dot on the "i" before we capitalize it and make something of ourselves.

It isn't easy, at first, getting our perceptions onto the page. We write grudgingly and under half steam, resentfully and uphill. "Who cares" and "This is stupid" are our companion thoughts. We don't want to take the time or trouble to record how it is we felt last night sitting in a community auditorium, listening to chamber music being played by gifted youngsters. We don't want to parse out if the something missing was in the music, in the playing, or in ourselves.

It takes an effort to be clear about things. It is easier and much sadder to be muddy, to never take the time to clarify our thoughts and connect—that word again—to our own perceptions. The act of paying attention is what brings us peace. In meditation we pay attention to the breath or to the image or to the mantra. We concentrate on something, and that concentration, that stillness, brings us to the point of knowing that we are all right, that God is in his heaven and all is right with the world—even if we believe in no God and no heaven. The act of concentration is that powerful, that filled with blessings. This is why I say that to begin with, we must connect.

It is an interesting question: "If I found myself and my thoughts interesting, what might I try?" We might discover we have a novel brewing that we have been too shy to unwrap. We might discover that we have a raft of paintings that are going unpainted lest we be "dull." We might discover that we are not putting to the page our one-woman show or our idea for a documentary film. If I were interesting, why, I might try any number of things. Piano lessons for the duration of my fifties, for example. Why not?

Why not? is the question that attention raises. I like this and I don't like that, and why not? I am trying this and I am not trying that, and why not? I could do this or I could do that, and why not? Connection brings us squarely to the issue of choice. There's a bright red post planted in the ground where we are standing. The post is our consciousness. We can go on from here in any number of ways, any number of directions.

From feeling nothing in particular, we have come to feel something very particular. From saying "It's no big deal," we have come to notice the many smaller "deals" we have made with ourselves, chief among them the deal not to take ourselves and our dreams seriously, because, after all, "Who do I think I am?"

That becomes the interesting question when we connect. Who *do* I think I am? Is that someone the same or different from yesterday? The same or different from my neighbor? Where am I and what do I think about that becomes something worth bothering about? The film that dulled our eyes and our vision and our image of ourselves gets clearer a swipe at a time. Every time we take pen to page we become more ourselves, less something vague and amorphous. We stumble onto our opinions and say, "Aren't you persnickety," but we begin to say it with interest and amusement. We are less the elderly cat sunning in the window and more the kitten with the ball of string, giving it a little bat to see where it goes.

"Where does this thought go?" We start to chase our consciousness a little. We are roused out of our torpor, our ennui. Life becomes a matter of some interest and we become the interested bystanders and then the participants. All of this happens because we connect. All of this happens a page at a time, a pen stroke at a time. SCRATCH. Start from scratch. Just move your pen across the page and watch what happens to you.

ATTENTION

Try this: Set aside one hour's writing time. You may wish to take yourself to neutral territory, a café or coffee shop. Once there, settle in to write and to describe yourself as you would a literary character, in the third person. Not "I am fifty-four years old" but "She is fifty-four years old." Describe your looks, your attitudes, your perceptions. Try to draw a clear portrait of yourself, filled with telling details. In other words, pay attention to how you are and how you are doing.

The Storm

THE SKY OVER THE HUDSON RIVER is dark green. In the Midwest this color sky means twisters. In New York it means big rain. Lightning bolts are dropping like jagged swords. A stiff, quick wind forces its way in my cracked-open windows, freshening the lace curtains. We are in for it, all the weather signs show. As luck would have it, I am going out. I am headed to the East Side, a forty-five-minute cab ride away. There I will see a read-through of a play by Rodgers and Hammerstein, one of their few failures, instructive for what it missed, not what "hit."

The lightning bolts remind me of how we think and talk about creativity. The way we speak in dramatic terms of "breakthroughs." We even use the phrase "bolt of insight." Every so often, just like tonight's big storm, I do get a creative breakthrough or a bolt of insight, but much more often creativity is pedestrian and nondramatic, more a matter of suiting up and showing up and listening than standing on the edge of the cliff as the earth splits open at my feet. I experience writing more like taking dictation than giving it. I try to write something down, not think something up, and the sense of direction is important here.

I think if we talked more realistically about what creativity feels like, we might let ourselves do a little more of it. If we thought of it as normal—98.6 on the human spectrum—instead of a sudden spike in our psychic temperature, we might let ourselves do it as a daily practice. We might all show up at the page or the easel and discover that there are reams of work waiting to move through us, right now, in the exact life that we have already. We might discover that creativity is not a marathon event that we must gird ourselves for, whacking off great swaths of life as we know it to make room for it.

Creativity is not aberrant, not dramatic, not dangerous. If anything, it is the pent-up energy of *not* using our creativity that feels that way.

This is the centenary year of Richard Rodgers's birth, and throughout the entire city and all around the world, events are going on that celebrate the daily practice Rodgers made of his own creative gifts. I have read books of his letters to his wife. They say, "I love you—and I am working." I have read his autobiography that says, "I love working." I have even read a particularly sour and mean-spirited biography of the man that also concludes: "He loved his work."

What all of this reading and focusing on Rodgers gives me is a sane model for what it is I try to do, showing up daily at both the page and the piano. I sit at the keys, seldom hearing any melody until I move my fingers across the keys and hear the melody locked within them. Nearly always, there is a song waiting to be written with words waiting to be sung. If I don't sit down at the piano, the song goes uncaptured. Perhaps it would visit again another day, perhaps not. It behooves me to have my butterfly net ready. And it is the same with words. The act of sitting down to the keys or to the lined page, the physical position of readiness, seems to cue the stream of thoughts to come forward now. I think the stream is always there, a current into which I tap at will. It is less a matter of "my" creativity than it is my being available to creativity. Something or someone wants to enter the world through us, and we are the portals that allow that entrance to take place.

Composers more than writers tend to acknowledge that music comes to them from a higher source of inspiration, that they are the gateways and not the source. The ego may rankle at first, but how much better to be the gateway for a large and mysterious something than the owner and guardian of a small and limited something, my "share" of creativity. I like knowing that there is something larger than myself, larger than all of us, that moves into the world when we are accessible to it as a conduit. I like having songs and stories come through me. I like knowing that my art is in a sense none of my business, not "my" art at all.

The sky is flooded with water and with light. It shines out like shook foil. Great claps of thunder rumble above the city. The skyscrapers are getting their parapets shampooed. It is a storm of storms. Something greater and grander than ourselves is having a time of it tonight, and I am glad. It draws things to scale. It makes it clear how my choice is to stand aloof from or to try joining this magnificent something that is so huge and so breathtaking and so certainly filled with power and light. How much better to say, "I am a part of all of this, hallelujah!" Better by far than laboring to make "my" great novel, "my" statement." Why not listen and write what seems to want to be written rather than writing all capital I's?

THE STORM

Try this: Nothing invites creative breakthroughs so successfully as walking. Even a
twenty-minute Walk is long enough to fling
open the inner door to insight and inspiration.
Take a twenty-minute Walk. Take note: What
ideas come to you? What insights, inspirations,
and realizations? We speak of a body of knowledge, and walking gives us access to exactly
that. We embody far more truth than we often
allow ourselves to contact. Walking puts us in
touch.

Gaining Through Loss

I WOKE THIS MORNING wrapped in loss. I was caught between sleep and waking, living again in a house that I had once lived in, loved, and lost—lost once and for all to a persistent and dangerous prowler whom we could not rout. Lying in my New York bed, in my New York bedroom, in the midst of my busy and productive New York life, I was back in New Mexico in my house full of saltillo tiles with the scratching sound of my pack of dogs as they waited eagerly for me to be up and with them for the day.

I once had five acres, seven horses, and seven dogs. I do not have them now. If I let myself, I miss every inch—apple trees, wooden fences constantly in need of repair, acequias gently slough-ing with water and stray twigs on our irrigation days. I miss every twitch, every hair of each of the dogs, given away, one at a time, to loving friends. I miss the silken muzzle of each horse, nuzzling me for an apple or carrot, saying, "That's it? Hay?" when I fed them each morning.

If I let myself, I cannot be in the now because I am overcome by the power of the then, the beauty and grace of all that I have left behind. But the prowler could not be caught by any known arm of the law, and it was too hard to stay on, sleeping at night with all of my dogs banked against danger, with every scratch of a twig at every window sending us all into high alert.

So I cannot let myself linger in that past.

I throw back the covers. I am in New York. I head to the kitchen and make a pot of strong British tea. I take a cup and retreat to the living room, where I put myself to the page. I start writing, and as I do, a sense of dailiness and normalcy returns. Gradually, I ebb back from that past house into this one. The apple trees outside my New Mexico windows are replaced by the American elms down in Riverside Park. The saltillo tiles give way to the parquet floors in this very nice apartment. Times have changed. The old house is gone. This is the new house. "It is all right," my writing tells me. "Life is not only bearable with loss. It is beautiful."

Life is beautiful, but we must have enough emotional equilibrium to experience it that way. If our inner resources are too meager, we must take action to restore them. It is too risky to blame life for our own lack of living. Life is full of sorrow, and sour, but it is also full of sweet.

For so many of us, it is hard to be both large enough and small enough to hold the range of life. Without a spiritual connection to something larger than ourselves, we lose our bearings, our beings, our sense of scale. Of course we do. The human experience is intricate, painful, and very beautiful. We lead lives filled with loss and filled with gain. Without a tool to metabolize what we live through—and for me that tool is Morning Pages—and even with it, it is hard to process who we have been and who we have become. So much happens to each of us. It is hard to make peace. Life is like the sea. A wave of memory sweeps in that threatens to overwhelm us and then the wave retreats, leaving us to wonder at what has been washed ashore.

Today I feel staggered by the power of my emotions, the pull of the past. Today I must work to have faith, to trust the newness

GAINING THROUGH LOSS

that has been made from my loss. To trust what has been put in place of all that went before. I must live, as the wise ones tell us, one day at a time. This means I must turn to my tool kit and pull from it the tool that has served me longest and best. I must write. One day at a time, I can chip away at the musical play that I am writing now.

One day at a time, I can love the two dogs I now share a life with, two rescues from lives as torn apart as my own. These new dogs are beautiful. I can work to make their lives stable and happy. I can give them walks, not along an acequia, not through the fragrant sage, but chasing squirrels along a stone wall in Riverside Park. It is enough. The present is big enough to hold the past. I must let the present enlarge enough to become rich and deep. I must live in it, not just occupy its time.

Morning Pages remind me that while I cannot choose much of what happens to me in my life, I can choose how I respond to what happens. The trick is getting small enough to inch forward. The past is huge. The future may be huge as well. What remains for me, what is given, is to do the small tasks of the day. First among those tasks is Morning Pages, the daily writing of three pages that draws me into the life I have now, the choices I can make today to find beauty in what is given to me.

· 35 ·

GAINING
THROUGH LOSS

Try this: Do not be surprised if you are resistant to this task. It is very powerful—so powerful that in many cultures, it is considered a religious act. I am talking about doll-making. Draw to mind a loss you wish to memorialize or transform. Now, using whatever materials strike you as appropriate, make a doll that reflects your many emotions. Some dolls involve frippery and finery. Others are made from twigs and sticks. You will know the right form for you, and it is that form you should choose to make. Be prepared for a powerful shift in consciousness.

Ripening

THE SKY IS A DULL, throbbing gray. It looks like rain but doesn't rain. Instead, the green buds on trees push palpably outward into bloom. A time-lapse photo of the park below my writing window would show a greener, leafier afternoon than morning.

We blossom just as the trees blossom, but we cooperate so much less. While the trees lean into the approaching seasons and submit themselves to the will of nature, we fight the richness being made of ourselves and we fight it with "busyness." Too many people, too many books, newspapers, and events, crowd our consciousness for our own ripening to occur. We are distracted from the matter at hand: another soul being brought into maturity.

Life rushes past us pell-mell. We book our days from morning to evening and then wonder why they lack succulence and savor. We go months, years even, without talking to once-cherished friends. We are too busy living a life to have a life worth living. Walk on the streets. How many strangers meet your eyes? We walk quickly, eyes averted, busy each with our own thoughts, and if someone looks at us directly, that is intrusive. We feel the same way about staring at someone we pass. We act as if we have no right to inhabit this life we are fully and certainly inhabiting. The passing parade must "pass"; we cannot be caught sucking on it like a candy lozenge to get its sweetness and taste.

I am alone today. My roommate has gone to Florida for two days, and the house is quiet except for the occasional restless stirring of one of the dogs. This morning at six-thirty, hours before I planned to be up, the smallest dog, Charlotte, a West Highland terrier, set up a frantic scratching at my bedroom door. She had decided the night was over, that it was time for company and cheer. Not from me it wasn't. When I emerged an hour later, unable to ignore her pleas, I discovered she had made good use of her time by savaging the contents of my purse, paying particular attention to a small bottle of allergy pills, which she had opened and scattered in parti-colored amulets across the living-room carpet. "All right, I will walk you," I all but snapped, fastening leashes to Charlotte and her companion, Tiger Lily, a cocker spaniel. Out we charged into the gray and luminous morning. The air in the park just off the Hudson was heavy with moisture. Daffodils and jonquils glowed like candles. It was beautiful to be up and out. No matter that the neighbors were still abed and the little park deserted.

I read most of the morning. I am rereading my friend Natalie Goldberg's books, cherishing her Technicolored prose, as vivid as salami on rye. Natalie grew up on Long Island in a split-level tract home where food was the focus of life, and food remains in her pages a focus for life and a token of how well or ill a life is being led. "Is it delicious?" Natalie's books are succulent, filled to bursting with colors and flavors. I am reading them to double-check myself—am I being authentic, real with myself, with what I think and what I have to say?

It is good to have some alone time. To drop down into my thoughts and into my life with no one expected home and noth-

ing required of me for a while. I can think about what I choose
and whom I choose. I can leaf through my Rolodex and phone
those friends who are missing in action—some of them for years.
Perhaps because I have lived a life in many places—New York, Los
Angeles, Chicago, Taos—I have led a disconnected life. I must
work to stay in touch with those who are near and dear to me
from each locale, and inevitably as I shift places, I shift friendships
with only the mail and e-mail to save me as I try to keep up a
stream of notes that say, "Still thinking of you, although you are
there and I am here."

In my friend Natalie's books, she makes frequent mention of
death—how it draws everything to scale and makes everything
living so much more beautiful and poignant. I am fifty-four years
old. I do not know how many more years I am allotted or how
long I will remain on this earth, which I love. I do know that I
do better being here when I try to be here consciously. To see the
same world with a stranger's eyes. To walk my neighborhood streets
as a visitor might, with a sense of wonder.

This afternoon I took myself for a brief walk. I stopped at a side-
walk table laden with books. One book—for ten dollars—was irresistible to me. It was a book on the origin of words. I love words
and handle them the way a baby does a first string of beads: each
one so bright and such a different color and shape! The little book
promised the origin of eight thousand words, among them "abyss"
(from the Greek "bottomless"). How could I not want to know?
This is what I wonder as I move through New York, crowded with
its all-but-faceless crowds: How could I not want to know?

I spend one third of the year in Taos, a tiny town of less than
five thousand people, and the rest of the year in New York, a

metropolis. In Taos I am a known face, and in New York I am a faceless face, one more amid many. In Taos I cherish the "known" faces that I see in restaurants, at the post office, at the copy shop, each of us on our rounds. In New York I cherish my anonymity as I make the same rounds. But in New York I am always wondering, "Who are you?" and it is the promise of the city with its many stories that keeps me coming back like an avid reader dazzled by the library shelves.

RIPENING

Try this: Go to a local five-and-dime or phar-
macy. Select five postcards that lend the place
you live a little magic. Set aside a half hour
and take the time to write out five cards to
far-flung friends and relatives. It's enough to
just say "thinking of you." Everyone likes to be
thought of.

To Be Independent,
Depend on God

IN THE DAYS when spiritual beliefs held more intellectual currency, it was routine for artists to speak of divine inspiration. Prayer was a part of everyday life and a working tool in an artist's repertoire. Writers prayed for plotlines, composers prayed for melody, painters prayed that their brush be guided. Masterpieces were the result.

In our modern lives, it can seem quaint, otherworldly, or unbelievable to ask for—and expect—divine guidance in our creative endeavors. We have lost the sense of God as a working partner. He is too distant and too busy for affairs like our own. With the crush of cities, the crowds pressing through the subway turnstile, the jostling bodies on a midtown street, it is easy to believe this assessment, and yet, is it valid?

Thomas, a young composer, seeks spiritual guidance daily. He asks for help, and he gets it—sometimes as a melody line, sometimes as the impulse to organize his arranging space. Each time he acts on the guidance received, goodness and creativity flow from his pen. For Thomas, asking for guidance is both a habit and a necessity. He takes great comfort in the spiritual forces he senses contact with. Composing is a lonely business, and it gives him a sense of companionship, praying for guidance and receiving it.

Nadine is an accomplished writer with many books to her

credit. For her, writing and prayer are intermingled. The act of writing is a sort of distillate. She begins each writing session with a conscious effort to empty herself, to be a vessel for divine thought to flow through her. And yet, Nadine is a funny writer, earthy and sensuous. Her spirituality has not neutered her prose.

Mitchell, a photographer, has been on a spiritual path for fifteen years. He considers his considerable career a collaboration between him and a higher power. Routinely, he asks for inspiration and guidance. He has traveled around the world, camera in hand, finding the hidden face of God in those who face his lens.

"God I believe, help my disbelief," prays Arthur, a distinguished writer. The author of more than a dozen books, Arthur asks guidance on each new endeavor, waiting to write until he feels a sense of rightness in a new direction. Not surprisingly, his career is notable for its originality and often unexpected directions.

Talk to enough artists, and the surprising fact emerges that praying for spiritual guidance results in originality, not sameness. We are inspired to become ourselves, as unique and multiple as the snowflakes.

TO BE
INDEPENDENT,
DEPEND ON GOD

Try this: Sometimes we are loath to rely on the
Great Creator. Perhaps we still believe in a difficult, negative, or withholding God. The kind
of God we believe in has a great deal to do
with our willingness to draw close to God. This
is a two-part exercise.

STEP ONE: Number from 1 to 10 and list ten
attributes of your childhood God. For example:

1. *Distant*
2. *Stern*
3. *Male*
4. *Humorless*
5. *Punishing*
6. *All-knowing*
7. *All-powerful*
8. *Prefers martyrs*
9. *Prefers suffering*
10. *Difficult to reach*

Now number from 1 to 10 again. This time, list the characteristics you would *like* your God to have. For example:

1. *Kind*
2. *Encouraging*
3. *Creative*
4. *Humorous*
5. *Easy to reach*
6. *Supportive*
7. *Enthusiastic*
8. *Adventurous*
9. *Personal*
10. *Interested*

STEP TWO: Holding in mind the positive traits you have envisioned, write a letter to God asking for specific help regarding your life and creative projects. You may wish to create a ritual related to this letter, placing it in a "God Jar" or on a small altar devoted to your creativity.

Wishes Come True

LIFE IS OUT OF OUR CONTROL—but not entirely. This morning, at the New-York Historical Society, I watched a short documentary film about the founding of New York. So many of today's complaints about New York can be traced back to the founding fathers' plans and wishes for it. It was to be a city of commerce, a moneymaking venture where the frippery of mere beauty was placed aside for the more urgent business of business.

In planning Manhattan, the founders chose to remove wildness from it, to flatten hills, ignore streams and gullies, restrict trees to borderline tracery, making greenery a rare sight except for Central Park, where the wildness and beauty of the original Manhattan Island survives, man-made but beguilingly intact. Thanks to the vision of city planners, chief among them De Witt Clinton, modern New York is built upon a grid, a grid envisioned and executed to give us what we have: straight streets with numbers instead of names, a city made easy to learn for immigrants who come here speaking a wide variety of tongues. Houses and public buildings are built—deliberately built—to stand shoulder to shoulder in neat, orderly rows, very democratic in their essential sameness. In downtown New York, the part of the city built before the city planners' version, the streets run at crooked angles and have names. South of Houston Street, once a northern border, New York is a tangle on a par with London and Paris, older cities that grew a neighborhood at a time, not with the topiary sameness and forced urgency of New York. We have all heard the phrase "Your wish is my command," and New York heard very clearly the city planners' wish to be an economic focal point, no mere spot of beauty.

Wishes are potent forces, not only for cities but for people. Like the city planners of old, all of us lead lives that we have subconsciously gridded out. A choice at a time, we execute our lives, placing into them what matters to us. We buy houseplants because we hunger for green life. We Windex our windows, yearning for more light. We may write down "next time, a sunnier apartment." We all have things we wish for more of, and we all carry with us wishes we have not articulated, even to ourselves. When we feel cut adrift, it is often because our unacknowledged wishes are crying for our attention and we are turning a deaf ear. At such times we need to take pen to the page and listen to the voices within us that want further expression in our lives. We must make our unconscious conscious. We must allow these voices to help us grid our growth or we will grow helter-skelter and not in directions that give us the soul satisfaction that we crave.

WISHES COME TRUE

Try this: Take pen in hand and lay out a wish list of 1 to 20. Allow your wishes to be what they are, to range from the minuscule and easily fulfilled to the large and seemingly impossible. Wishes address the quality of our life and the contents of what we put into life's container. When we put our wishes to the page, we tend to act on those that are easily accessible to us and to be available when the large gears of the universe swing into place and offer us something we have felt lies beyond our reach.

Happy Accidents

YESTERDAY, making a demo disc for a musical, we ran across an unexpected problem: The music was too complex and demanding to be recorded accurately and well in the time we had at hand. The studio clock was ticking. Money was being spent instant by instant, tick by tock. With the pressure rising, the singers were still stubbornly out of tune, missing notes and making discordant errors. Something had to be done. Reluctantly and angrily, my creative partner and I shifted gears. All right, we would lose our large and grand choral opening. We would open instead with our closing—a sprightly, upbeat, and far simpler musical medley. We hated to do it. But when we did it, the demo disc jumped alive.

Accidents happen, and when they do and we are willing to roll with the punches, our creativity springs up and takes a turn. "Just let me see what I can make from this," the inner creator says. "There must be a silk purse in here somewhere." When we are willing to be open-minded, silk purses abound. They are the "found art" of life, the opportunity waiting to be seized by the optimists among us. Rather than focusing on our losses, we can learn to focus on our "founds." We can see what unexpected resource a loss calls to the fore. We can see how our being flexible and open to alternative solutions can offer us not just different but better solutions to what it is we attempt. We may not like looking for it, but we can find the silver lining. Let me give you a case in point.

When I was a single mother, undisturbed writing time was at a premium. I was with my daughter 24/7, and she was a lively, inquisitive child not prone to napping. From this I learned to get up early and spring to the page before my daughter needed me. This is how Morning Pages came to be born. I also learned, when she was a toddler, how to write through distractions like an afternoon's cartoon show or a rigorous game of hobby horse racketing through the apartment. Because I had to write whenever I could and however I could, my writing, of necessity, became portable and doable. I hauled a notebook with me and wrote in school corridors, in doctors' waiting rooms, anywhere and anytime I had a moment. As a direct result, art became something casual and daily. I well learned that plays were written a sentence at a time, because sometimes that was all I got on the page before a parent/teacher meeting, before the school bus pulled up and my daughter stepped down, needing a snack and her mommy.

Unlimited time became the luxury I yearned for, but because I didn't have it, time became what I learned to use. A minute here and a minute there and there was, surprisingly, "enough" of it. I just had to be willing to be open-minded. I just had to be willing to give up my agenda of "lots" of time, my fantasy of life as a full-time artist, and settle for the patchwork quilt of time here and time there.

My daughter is twenty-five now, and I sometimes have the luxury of time, but in the music studio yesterday, we recorded one song that I wrote waiting in a parking lot and another that came to me as I drove crosstown through Los Angeles traffic. Sam Shepard has said that he writes on highways. Gertrude Stein composed poems at the wheel of her parked car. If we are open to our art, our art will seize whatever opening we give to it.

When we are willing to be open-minded, art and beauty come flooding into us in a thousand small ways. When we let ourselves see the possibilities instead of the improbabilities, we become as flexible and resilient as we really are. It is human nature to create. When we cooperate with our creativity, using it to live within the lives we actually have, we surprise ourselves with our level of invention. The closing medley becomes the opening medley. Today's snatched sentence opens the new play.

HAPPY ACCIDENTS

Try this: Choose one situation in your life about which you feel negative. Take fifteen minutes for yourself. With pen in hand, explore the possible positives you stand to gain through this situation. For example: "Your play seems almost like two one-acts yoked together."

The possible positive is moving some of the action of Act II into Act I, thus linking the two halves far more closely together. This shift creates foreshadowing in Act I for Act II. The play now reads as a cohesive whole, because you were willing to accept and act on constructive criticism.

Befriending Time

TODAY WAS UNSEASONABLY WARM. Manhattan was in shirt-sleeves and wide, loony grins. The weather had everyone happily tilted toward optimism and friendliness. Old couples strolled arm in arm, beaming at those striding toward them. Children clutched helium balloons bought on the street. Lovers walked intertwined and heedlessly erotic: her hand in his back pocket. A West Highland terrier, out for a morning constitutional, assumed a stubborn, leg-braced "Westie position" and refused to be dragged indoors from the glorious day. What is it about spring that wakes up the artist in all of us? We suddenly have "the time" of our lives—a telling phrase.

People take walks on their lunch hours. Passersby impulsively stop to pet the small black cocker spaniel puppy making his brave way down Columbus Avenue, owner in tow. Stores leave their doors ajar and owners loll against the doorjambs, making casual conversation with neighbors walking by. The clock is banished. Oscar Hammerstein had it right: "I feel so gay in a melancholy way . . ."

Spring opens a trapdoor in the mind of many of us. It allows that creative imp Impulse to slip in. Rather than glancing at our watch and hurrying ahead to our next "jump" on a busy agenda, we pause, dazzled by the bright flowers banked up outside a Korean grocer's. "Aren't they beautiful?" we ask a complete stranger.

"Indeed they are," he replies, his English accent a pleasant added treat.

So much of art hinges on our ability to trust intuition, to follow our hunch about what "might" or "could" come next. The difference between a blocked artist and a free one is this precise openness to moment-by-moment invention. Agnes de Mille tells us that an artist must take "leap after leap in the dark." Picasso tells us that we are all born children, "the trick is remaining one." How do we remain one? Having the time of our lives is the answer. Being open to the right timing of coincidence is the key.

We live in the now, where children and animals live. We learn to stop watching the inner movie—the movie of "How am I and how is my brilliant career?"—long enough to take a lively interest in the people and things around us. Children are dazzled by a butterfly, entranced by a floating leaf, utterly captured by the sight of an unexpected horse trotting briskly along the roadside. When our adult self is too much in evidence, we "notice" such diversions but we do not allow ourselves to be diverted, turned aside from the serious business of life. We dampen our own enthusiasms lest they lure us from the path of our ambitions. Focused on our ambitions and the way they "should" unfold, we often miss the way they are unfolding, or are trying to if only we would let them.

The word *enthusiasm* comes from the Greek words meaning "filled with God." If, as Mies van der Rohe is said to have remarked, "God is in the details," maybe we belong there as well. Maybe the most direct route to our heart's desires is a circuitous one that allows us to encounter destiny by stopping to admire the calico cat sunning itself amid the geraniums on a window ledge.

Perhaps those shortcuts that cut out the sweetness of life are really cutting us off from life itself.

Henry Miller advised us, "Develop interest in life as you see it; in people, things, literature, music—the world is so rich, simply throbbing with rich treasures, beautiful souls and interesting people. Forget yourself. . . ."

It is one of the ironies of opening ourselves to impulse that we not only forget ourselves—our serious workaday selves—but we discover ourselves, our luminous, "incandescent" selves. Is it too radical to consider that Brenda Ueland might just be on the right track when she urges us: "Think of yourself as an incandescent power, illuminated and perhaps forever talked to by God and his messengers."

Certainly spring, which "springs" us from the cage of our wintry selves, makes this an easier notion to entertain. Daft with the weather, we talk to ourselves and one another—"Oh, what a beautiful morning. Oh, what a beautiful day!" Perhaps Something is talking to us and we are merely answering.

I believe that we live in an interactive universe, that we are being talked to and responded to at all times. Everything is significant, not just the few somethings that we allow ourselves to see when we are blinded by our blind ambition.

BEFRIENDING TIME

Try this: For most of us, time is what we feel we never have enough of. We don't have time to call an old friend and get current with each other. We don't have time to go for a walk. We don't have time to take a leisurely bubble bath. We serve quick-fix meals rather than take the time to make a real salad and broil some fish. We even choose our clothes by looking for those that require no time.

Take pen in hand and number from 1 to 10. List ten activities that you would enjoy but tell yourself you have no time for. Don't these neglected possibilities sound self-nurturing? They are, of course, and that is why we need to find the time to do them. Select one self-nurturing action from your list. Make the time to execute it.

Easy Does It

A CLOSE EXAMINATION of many an artistic career reveals that "genius" is often coupled with plain ordinary work. A case in point? Richard Rodgers. A daily worker, he built not only his career but his entire life on a firm foundation of "easy does it."

The auditorium was white and small with white Doric columns, and velvet wall hangings in burgundy. The crowd was notably amiable for a New York theater crowd, smiling and nodding, settling in comfortably. We were there to listen to little-known Richard Rodgers songs. As the lights dimmed, Rodgers's elder daughter, Mary, took her place toward the front, a genial, silver-haired woman who bears a striking resemblance to her father.

The program began with a few cordial bromides and then got down to business—show business. With three singers alternating solos and pairing up for duets, the evening moved through the lesser-known areas of Rodgers's works. The composer of nine-hundred-plus songs, he left a lot of musical territory behind him. As famous as his works are, we are familiar with only the tip of the iceberg of his output.

All of us who make things worry whether or not what we make is "original." Listening to the Rodgers evening proved this worry to be irrelevant. Clearly, Rodgers was the "origin" of all his work. The prism of his sensibility is what made it original. The same is true for all of us. We are the origin of our work. Our

THE SOUND OF PAPER

allowing work to move through us is the issue. As we suit up and show up each day at the page or easel or the camera, we have an "eye" that becomes the "I" present in all that we do.

Rodgers liked to work every morning. He got to the piano by nine or nine-thirty and put in his time there in the same way an assembly-line worker would punch a time clock. He left the door to the room ajar, and his daughters remember tiptoeing through the house during their father's work time.

Rodgers's output was prodigious, but on closer examination, it was simply steady. He worked at his work. It was his lifeline and his through line. It was what he did, whether it was going well or poorly, whether it was well received or ill received. Every day, rise and shine, regardless of his emotional weather, he went to the piano and listened there for the work that would move through him. Allowing that work to enter the world, resigning from judging its caliber—leave that to history—Rodgers wrote note after note, day after day, leaving us with a legacy of work and a legacy of how to work—steadily and without ego.

From all available sources, we can conclude that Rodgers was not a happy man. He struggled with depression and with alcohol, and even so, he worked. Linked for twenty-odd years to lyricist Larry Hart—until death did them part—and later to Oscar Hammerstein, Rodgers had a gift for devotion, and nowhere was this more apparent than in his daily giving himself over to the work. Sometimes he wrote for high-minded musicals. Sometimes he wrote for rollicking revues. The point is that he wrote, always, and that in doing so he left an example of how it is we can work as well. Some of the best work came during the darkest times. Some of the brightest times did not burnish the work. The work became a separate entity, an ongoing something that had its own life and its own rules, chief among them, "Be loyal to me."

Rodgers had a marathon marriage to his beloved wife, Dorothy. "I have loved that woman for forty years," he once exclaimed. But if Dorothy was his wife, his even deeper marriage was to his work. As Dorothy herself wrote, introducing a volume of his love letters, "It wasn't easy for me to accept the fact that I wasn't the most important thing in Dick's life. His work was. I was, I think, the most important person in his life, but his work was, quite simply, his life."

Richard Rodgers did not write all day, every day. He wrote first thing in the morning, when he was fresh. When the work hours were over, then he was husband, father, and friend. Listening to his lesser-known songs, hearing in them the same talent that would make so many of his other songs recognizable standards, it is clear that Rodgers took to heart the fact that he was the "origin" in original. In some ways less a person than a place, he met his destiny daily at the piano and allowed the work to move through him, stormy weather or clear.

EASY DOES IT

Try this: Most of us imagine that if we had an emptier life and more money, we would get more done. The truth is that such a life invites distractions, and we do much better to work with the life we have. The art of living in the now requires that we be alert to the choices of the moment, that we use our time well. Twenty minutes is enough time for a short walk, a luxurious bath, or piano practice. If we allow ourselves to take an "easy does it" approach and content ourselves with progress rather than perfection, we can find many arenas in which we can take small strides. Take pen in hand. List five areas of your life in which you would like to see "improvement." Next to each area, write a small, forward-looking action that you *could* take. For example:

> *Playing the piano: twenty minutes of daily practice can be shoehorned into the busiest life.*

You get the idea: Easy does it, but do it.

Staying in Condition

THE DAY IS GRAY AND TURBULENT. West winds send high gusts through the streets. For anyone, but especially for someone with hair like mine, it is a bad hair day. I have a great deal of very fine, very unmanageable hair. It has always been like this. In a passport picture taken in my twenties, I look like an Irish terrorist. (Why are terrorists always distinguished by their unkempt, uncontrollable hair?) I have learned that my hair can be managed if I invest time and care in it. If I go to the hairdresser, once a week at best, and have my hair slathered with moisturizers and deep conditioners, then it will cooperate and give an impression of civility for a few days. I can use those few days if I need to have a portrait taken or make a speech. This week I am making a speech. Tomorrow afternoon I will get on a train, leave New York, and travel south a few speedy hours to Washington, D.C. I went to school in Washington, back when I looked like a terrorist, and I am hoping for a more kempt arrival and appearance.

One of the things my mass of ne'er-do-well hair has taught me is that there are some things that do better if we don't let them get away from ourselves. Too many days without conditioner and my hair is a tangled mess. Too many days without writing and my syntax tangles too. I write daily, and I do it not because I am virtuous but because it is easier that way, more manageable. Writing is still difficult enough. It is still a steep hill: Choose a topic to write about and then make a series of further choices, word by word, until your topic is "covered." When I was younger, before I had learned the hair trick, I hadn't learned the writing trick either. In those days I wrote in spurts of fancy, yanking at my prose to get a comb through it once a week or so. Not writing enough, I would begin writing knotted up already. There were too many thoughts vying for attention. There was too much pressure to find the "right" way to write. I would dash at the page and before long tear my hair out: Why was writing such a jumble? Why was it so hard? Why was I so . . . stupid, cowardly—the pejorative word of the day?

In the days when women had crowning glories instead of short, businesslike bobs, they would brush their hair nightly, a hundred long, smooth strokes. Those strokes did for shine and maneuverability what conditioners and shine products do now. The application of a little simple elbow grease brought sheen and suppleness. Every woman was her own hairdresser, and well-dressed hair was well addressed by the nightly hundred strokes.

I don't know why it is that we fail to talk about art in terms of humble diligence. So much of making a career as an artist consists of the small strokes, the willingness to show up and try on a daily basis. So much of being good at something consists of being practiced at something so that the sudden gusts of a deadline blowing into your work space doesn't turn you into a terrorist, wild-haired and wild-eyed, unable to muster muscle and nerve enough to simply stick to the page. As artists, we can make our work daily and doable enough that we give it its daily measure of time and consistency. We can "show up" for our artist and, if we do, when we call on it, our artist will show up for us.

STAYING
IN CONDITION

Try this: Most of us have areas of our life that require daily upkeep. We may be writers, painters, sculptors, photographers, poets, film-makers, or dancers. Each of these activities can loom at us large and undoable if we allow ourselves to get away from the doing. Take pen in hand. Number from 1 to 5 and list five areas of your life that require—or would benefit from—daily maintenance. The ritual of a short nightly bedtime story may mean everything to a child. One home-cooked meal a day may mean a great deal to a spouse. The daily habit of writing something will mean the world to our writer. My mother swept her kitchen floor daily. I can put aside ten minutes to clean the kitchen before bedtime. If we don't let our life get away from us, we will have a life more worth husbanding.

Buds

THE WINDOW WHERE I WRITE overlooks Riverside Park. It is a dim day in late spring, and the park hovers between seasons. It is chilly if you are out there walking. It is seductively slightly green if you are inside looking out. The trees are frothed with the lightest tint of green.

Just like the weather, I am in between seasons, newly done with writing a long, hard wintry book and not yet awake to the fruitful summer of leisurely writing time that lies in front of me. Like the spring trees, I am putting out buds, the promises of future work. My short daily essays are the buds I put on bare branches. If I am alert enough and an optimist, I see these buds and know that something rich is coming in. I am experienced enough to know that the light-green misting promises full foliage and real ideas that will emerge just as surely as the trees below my window will be heavy with green before too long. It is hard, as an artist, to live with the seasonality of work and of mood. It is too easy to feel when each season's work ends. "That's it. It will never come again." This is one reason that seasoned artists like to devise ways to keep gently working.

Today I had lunch with my daughter, an actress. She is finishing a longish run in a well-received play, and when the show closes next week, she faces her first unscheduled downtime in nearly eight months. She has been asked to go to Idaho and do a play there, but she wants to stay in New York, where the action is. She is too young to believe, as I do, that the action is everywhere and the play in Idaho might be as dead center and important an experience for her as anything happening in SoHo. And so she will stay in New York and hope and worry until she is hired again. I sympathize but I think that it is dangerous to let our creative futures lie too firmly in the hands of others, even the Fates.

Creativity lies in the doing and not in the done. As artists, we all sense this but often forget it. Writers need to keep writing in between writing assignments, in between projects. Actors need to act, whether at acting class or by preparing a piece for open mic. Fine artists need to keep their hand sketching. A painter called me yesterday to tell me excitedly about a visit she had had with a master painter and the advice he had given her.

"What was it?" I asked.

"He told me to paint," she reported breathlessly. "Not to paint just what I had to paint but to also paint what I wanted to paint, to paint just anything, anything at all, that that would keep me from going stale and dried up."

Artists who do not keep playing at their art run a very real risk of going stale and dried up. The writer who writes a hard book and screeches to a halt, exhausted, runs the risk of writer's block— a block of time where anything feels easier than writing. The painter who paints only on commission runs the same risk and a corollary one: "I am not a 'real' artist; I'm a hired gun."

It is the making of art when we feel that we have no art in us that makes an artistic career. It is the pages logged when the well feels dry, the painting painted when the palette is parched, the monologue learned "for no damn reason" that keeps the gears turning. Ditto for the fine-arts photographer who loads a camera and takes to the streets even though the "real" work is in the carefully lit studio, as calculated as a NASA shot.

Goethe told us, "Whatever you think you can do or believe you can do, begin it. Action (boldness) has magic, grace and power in it." What better advice to the playwright who is in between plays with just the inkling of an idea? What good words for the novelist who is toying with a rare short-story idea. In between ideas, I wrote an entire album of children's animal songs and another time an album filled with flower songs—so doing the "slight" ideas we have adds up to longer ideas, often very good ones.

As artists, we do well to be a little like a profligate gardener, scattering a profusion of seeds and not weeding too closely at first. My book *The Artist's Way* began as tiny essays, the thoughts grabbed on the run before a class or after an afternoon's schoolwork with my daughter. The book grew an essay at a time, a thought at a time, because that was all I had time for and, besides, I wasn't "really" writing—but I was.

An artist moves through life like a thresher. Great swaths of experience get mowed down and churned up and spewed back out as art. Our job is so often just to keep the gears moving, let the scythe of our experience pass across the field of life, let the cuttings be what they are—books, songs, paintings, poems, the passing glories of each day's gentle march.

BUDS

Try this: Put on a pair of comfortable walking shoes. Give yourself forty-five minutes for a good ramble. Take yourself out of the house and onto the trail. It can be city or country; time matters more than locale. As you walk, hold lightly in mind an area of your work that you consider to be "in bud"—the beginning stages. Use your Walk to explore and expand the dimensions of the area you're interested in. You may walk out with the seed of a story and walk back in with an idea in full flower.

What If

THE SEASON IS AS BEAUTIFUL as a young girl turning into a woman. It has that same mix of newness and ripening. The magnolia trees are budding. The fruit trees in Riverside Park display a froth like Parisian petticoats. It is a day to flirt with alternate lives, with the thrill of possibility, and with life itself. One of my favorite creativity tools is the one that asks "What if?" What if I had five other lives to lead? What would I do in these imaginary lives? What would be fun to do?

My list is always long on whimsy about which I am dead serious. I write, "Be a torch singer." I write, "Be a composer." I write, "Be a flautist." In the life I have now, unless I am alert, music is often marginalized. I do not go to my piano often enough to just noodle. I let my perfectionist intrude, warning sternly, "You'd better be good at this if you are going to try it. . . ."

All of us carry an inner perfectionist. (A critic, a cynic, a skeptic, a censor. Name it what you will.) I call mine Nigel, and there is no pleasing him. Nigel is a thin-lipped critic, with his arms folded across his bony chest. Nigel demands to be shown my right to pursue an interest. Nigel wants me to be serious and good and seriously good. Nigel is the watchdog of great art, although I doubt that Nigel has ever let himself make very much of it. He is far too high-strung for mere dabbling and far too self-important for the idea of play.

Nigel is the one who snorts in derision when I think about starting a new play. Nigel is the one who is afraid to send finished work out—and is afraid, for that matter, to finish work because then it can be judged and people like him do the judging. Nigel was never formally invited to join my inner cast but somehow slunk in like a shadow, slithering through the cracks of consciousness and making himself right at home in the living room—not that he approves of the decor.

Nigel. I would like to lock you out. In one of my imaginary lives I have a virus sweeper installed in my household, and that virus sweeper makes fast work of any Nigels trying to get through the door or in the window. In that imaginary life I wear a small crucifix that wards Nigel off and I chew savory cloves of garlic that I breathe in Nigel's general direction. No Nigel sinks his pointed fangs into the jugular of my work in a next lifetime. In this imaginary lifetime I am an exorcist. I have Nigel handled.

WHAT IF

Try this: This is a surprisingly powerful though whimsical tool. Take pen in hand and number from 1 to 5. List five imaginary lives. Be careful to choose lives that sound fun to you. Referring to your list, take pen in hand again and list five actions you could take in the life you currently have to draw you closer to each of your imaginary lives. For example, if you have an imaginary life that says "cowboy," you can schedule a riding lesson. You can buy a book on horses. You can go to a horse show or rodeo. You can explore a dude ranch vacation. You can ride in a horse-drawn cab or pet a police horse. Anytime we take an action that resonates with an imaginary life, we feel better, somehow more ourselves.

For Art's Sake

LAST NIGHT, the Jewish Repertory Theatre, housed in the Center for Jewish History, presented *Two by Two,* a musical about Noah and the ark. Richard Rodgers wrote the music, and the staged reading of the show was a part of the ongoing Rodgers centennial festivities. The center is a modern building featuring postmodern security measures. Pockets were emptied, purses were searched, bodies lightly brushed by a sensing device on the prowl for explosives in the wake of the rash of suicide bombers striking in Israel. Just getting into the theater was a half-hour ordeal that everyone dealt with patiently and nervously: The day's headlines made impatience both naive and politically incorrect. At last, the play began.

The cast was dressed all in black, and the stage was dressed in black too. The only color came from the words and songs, and they were vibrant. The small show sprang to astounding life—and after only four days of rehearsals. For the better part of three hours, the audience was transported first to the ark and then to the world of relationships within Noah's family—the sorrow, the bickering, the disappointment, the love. The show's book was by Peter Stone, and it was a good one. The lyrics, by Martin Charnin, were charming, but the music, oh, the music by Richard Rodgers was melodic, persuasive, full-bodied, and glorious. He had, quite simply, done it again. "It" being tapped into a vein of melody and mined it for our joy.

No one was going to get famous performing the thirty-year-old show in front of a tiny house audience. The actors brought love and not ambition to their playing—or if ambition was present, it was doffed at stage right to be picked up again after the show. Stripped down to its essentials, the tiny troupe was suddenly archetypal—the traveling players who amused European courts and villages, the gypsy vagabonds who traveled by caravan, entertaining as they went.

New York can be an intimidating city. It is full of the best and the brightest, the largest and the top. But it is also full of the smallest and the simplest, the clearest and the purest. It is not hard, in New York, to gather a group of Broadway caliber to put up a small show of the type we were seeing. Broadway talent lives in New York, and it cannot always work on Broadway, so it works where it can.

A friend of mine is a Broadway singer who lives in New York as casually and as fully as in a small village. He knows what is going on everywhere and he gets to a startling amount of it. The other night he attended not one but two events, the first a group of octogenarian actors reminiscing about their art, the second an evening of song dedicated to the creator, dead for thirty years now. Perhaps because both celebrity and anonymity are so much a part of New York, the city remembers. Streets are labeled for Duke Ellington, Edgar Allan Poe, and Rodgers and Hammerstein. Apartments bear plaques: "*Rhapsody in Blue* was written here. In the C apartment line on an upright piano." If New York is about making it, there is a dignity in New York to *trying* to make it. Since trying is where the vast majority will end up, that had better be good enough. And it is.

FOR ART'S SAKE

Try this: Go to the five-and-dime and acquire a scrapbook. Now is the time to cherish your art for art's sake. Add to your scrapbook any mementos you have gathered up. Take the time to write a short longhand progress report. Date it and include it in your book. If you have a camera at hand, photograph yourself and your project "in process." "Here I am, practicing my piano," "Here we are at a rehearsal," "This is my trusty typewriter," "This lump of clay is the beginning of a sculpture." When we take time and attention to focus on our progress, we see that progress has been made. We add just a jot to our self-worth. Yes, we are working artists.

Teachability

THE MAN BENDS OVER his desk full of dials, taps a few keys, and squints at a computer screen. His expertise is sound. He is mixing a demo—ours. My creative partner and I have done two demos this year, and now we have samples of two of our musicals ready for any willing ears. We have put in long days with this sound expert, Scott Lehrer, and listened as he tuned our work, orchestrating not only the sound of music but the sound of silence. The precise interval of space between songs on a CD is an art unto itself.

Working with a master at sound is a little like discovering that you are color-blind—he hears things that you are deaf to. The normal human ear does not distinguish fine gradations of sound that are large and looming issues to him. The lick of a lip, the slight inhalation of a breath, the imperceptible pop of a "P"—he hears all of this and more. The one note out of six that is off-key jars his ear like a blaring horn: "That bass of yours again," he says. And he is right. What must it be like to hear with such a level of acuity? What must the basso ostinato of the subway sound like?

I am used to being the relative master of my trade. I have put thirty-five years into writing. I like to think—and sometimes think—it shows. In the sound studio I am a novice, a beginner. I cannot hear all that is being heard, and if I can hear something, I have to force myself to speak up, intimidated as I am by the gentle prowess of the man at the dials. "What do you think?" he will ask occasionally, and I will have to work to put into language what for me are still ephemeral impressions. There is no black and white here, like fixing a muddy sentence. It is, instead, a question of muddy *sound,* of the slightest differences—or so they sound to me. Something will sound "right" to me or "wrong," but I cannot quite say why. I have to force myself to say, "I like the second take better." I cannot always assign a reason to my liking one take over another. I am in over my head.

In the midst of all the microphones, the soundproofed walls, the switches, dials, levers, and monitors, I have an attack of gratitude. I am delighted with myself that I am willing to be an amateur here. It is a sign of health to me that I have come far enough in my art to know when there are others who can take me further and to be willing to defer to them. After many years of soldiering on alone, I am learning to be a team player and I am liking it. After so many years of closing out the voices and objections of others so that I could stay single-minded enough and single-pointed enough to finish books, I am now inviting input and finding it welcome.

If the first rule of magic is containment, knowing how not to and when not to talk about a project, I am now squarely in phase two, when talking about a project and listening about a project is valuable—largely new territory for me. After years of fighting off the unwelcome remark, I am learning when remarks are welcome—and useful. This feels like growth to me. I have become teachable.

For all of us, it is a delicate dance knowing when to be stubborn in our knowing and when to be open to input and others' knowing. We cannot make art by consensus. On the other hand, we do not always need to lead, to inaugurate, and to initiate. Having done that, having laid the track out of a first draft, we have to be open for input and improvement, and it may come to us, as mine currently does, in the form of other experts commenting from their strengths with no agendas of their own except good work. If I feel small and displaced in the face of such experience and expertise, that is my kettle of fish to deal with—and I deal with it by being vulnerable rather than defensive, by saying "I don't understand" rather than "I see."

"I don't understand" is not a bad place to be in artistically. Mystery and humility can enter through this willing doorway, and mystery and humility as much as mastery and egotism are the handmaidens of great art.

TEACHABILITY

Try this: The artist soul thrives on adventure. Many adventures require that we muster the courage to be a beginner. That bicycle trip to France requires that I haul out my bike and start riding. That black-and-white photography course says, "Get out the camera; shoot a few rolls." Yoga for beginners requires that I stretch myself physically and mentally. Attendance at an open mic invites me to bring a poem. Life is filled with adventure if we are openhearted. Take pen in hand. List five things you would love to do, if you didn't have to do them perfectly.

1. *If I didn't have to do it perfectly, I'd try*
   _____.

2. *If I didn't have to do it perfectly, I'd try*
   _____.

3. *If I didn't have to do it perfectly, I'd try*
   _____.

4. *If I didn't have to do it perfectly, I'd try*
   _____.

5. *If I didn't have to do it perfectly, I'd try*
   _____.

In Between

It is a dreary, gray day. Spring is still struggling to tug itself forward. So am I. Outside my writing window, it is drizzling, and my mood matches the atmosphere—dribs and drabs of depression, a light misting of malaise. What's wrong with me is what's wrong with spring: I am not all here yet. Some part of me is still caught in yesterday's winter, and that chill grip on my ankle will not let go.

For an artist, "I don't know" is the hard time. It is the season between seasons when you are not sure what you are making and if you are making anything worthwhile. All artists go through seasons of rooted joy and seasons of rootless restlessness and doubt. It goes with the territory. If we knew, always, what it is we know, there would be no new land to push forward to. We would do and redo what it is we do—and that is not the artist's life. Ours is a life of invention.

Invention demands that we expand our creative horizons. This is not always comfortable. We are called to write, paint, dance, and sculpt new territories. We are asked to explore new forms, to willingly relinquish the old, safe, and familiar. In short, we are asked to be explorers, pioneers, traveling always toward and past the known rim of our universe.

Right now I am inventing an opera about Magellan. He is a man who set off into unknown seas, sailing west to go east, looking for a strait that would lead through the newly discovered Americas and onward to the Spice Islands. Magellan's voyage cost him his life, although he did circumnavigate the globe. Sometimes, writing about Magellan, I wonder how costly my voyage in pursuit of him will prove. So far, it is five years and counting of writing, and nearly daily another song comes to me, expressing some other part of what I intuit the Master Mariner heard or saw. I do not suppose, working on *Magellan,* that this is a project for which there are long lines waiting to buy tickets. Maybe there will be, maybe there won't. My job as creator is to create regardless of outcome, regardless of doubt, despair, discomfort. My job, and I do not always like it, is to imitate the season unfurling outside my window and to push on through the gray into greater blossoming.

IN BETWEEN

Try this: "Curiosity is the mother of invention,"
it is said correctly. Most of us have topics we'd
love to know more about, but the pursuit of that
"more" can feel daunting. Take yourself to a
good children's bookstore. Choose one topic
you are curious about, say, dogs. Seek out a book
on dogs—their breeds, their habits, their ances-
tors. A children's book is often a wonderful place
to start to satisfy an adult curiosity. There are
books on engines, books on stars, books on rep-
tiles, fish, and birds. Allow yourself to locate at
least two books that speak to your curious soul.

Compassion

LAST NIGHT, in a light drizzle, I took a cab across town to the York Theatre, Fifty-fourth and Lexington. I went there to watch a read-through of *Androcles and the Lion,* a musical made initially for television, for which Richard Rodgers did both the lyrics and the music. My favorite song, the one worth the price of admission, was something sung by Androcles to the lion in which he exhorts the great and hungry beast to have a "velvet paw" and treat him gently. As the story goes, the great cat has been wounded. A large, sharp thorn has pierced its paw, and Androcles can extract the thorn and alleviate the beast's suffering only if the lion will be gentle enough for the extraction to work, only if the lion will have a "velvet paw."

Sometimes, as an artist, I want life to have a "velvet paw." I am willing to deal with the pain of life if it will just hold still for a moment and let me get the first gasp of the extraction over with. I can write about death and longing and loss, and it can all be real as a paper cut if I have the first beat of compassion for myself, a compassion that I ask life to extend to me but that I might do better to extend toward myself. "How brave you are," I might practice saying, instead of "Oh, you coward, look at how long it took you today to even try to write."

I am brave, but it is late. It is gathering dark outside my writing-room window. The lights across the Hudson are shimmering on the water. The waters themselves mirror back the darkening evening sky. I have put off writing today because I am in the beginning of knowing something I do not want to know, and writing will make that clearer to me. Making a piece of art always makes us clearer, more whole, and able to accept what life is handing down—and at the moment life is handing down an unpalatable truth. I am facing down a large lie that I have told myself—and as many others as would listen.

I am fifty-four years old, twice married, and twice divorced. I have lived for far longer stretches by myself and celibate than I would ever have believed possible or practicable. When I look in the mirror I see a still-pretty woman who looks finely drawn, stretched a little too tightly across her own bones. I look imperious, and if I don't have some humanizing touch in the near future I just might end up being as chilly and cool as the marble statues I so closely resemble. "A classical profile," I have always been told. I was photographed as a young woman with my hair atop my head and my neck wreathed in pearls. In photographs now, I look queenly, aristocratic, and ever so slightly haughty—this is not how I planned on ending up. I wanted to be one of those softer, more sensuous women, like my friend Dori, burnished by touch into looking heavier but still succulent with age. I don't look that way.

When my last husband told me two days ago that he had just remarried, I was surprised that I felt not relief, not "Oh, thank God, now he's her problem," but, instead, an onrush of what could only be called lust. For nine years and counting I have held a frosty reserve that I was better off without him. Now, now that he was irrevocably lost to me, I suddenly remembered all he had been to me, the sweet physicality, the beauty of his arm, his shoulder, the bridge of his nose. I remembered the taste of him, the weight of him, the sheer male animal glee he took in making love. Yes, he was a large man and he had held me, in our day, with a velvet paw. I remembered all of this. Tears bit my eyes and my breath caught.

What I like about art is the very thing that makes people fear it. It enlarges us. I am a better and more honest woman for having taken to the page today and admitted my locked-away feelings of the years. I am larger and better and softer and kinder and more open than I was resisting knowing what I knew. It is always this way with art. We say the unsayable and in saying it we name not only ourselves but also the human condition. By being willing to characterize our lives in art, we begin to have the character necessary to make living itself an art. We rise to the occasion that life offers us. I like the woman better who admits to missing and still desiring a former husband than I liked the woman who pretended so well that she was above caring for him since he had been the one who walked out.

COMPASSION

Try this: Most of us have been braver than we know, braver than we acknowledge. Take pen in hand and write yourself a fan letter, thanking and praising yourself for your courage. Be specific. "It was brave of you to go back to graduate school. It was brave of you to help your sister through her divorce. It was brave of you to submit an entry to a juried show. It was brave of you to take up fly-fishing." Your inner artist is proud of you for your many accomplishments. Let this letter be a place to share that pride. Write fully and fondly, then mail yourself the letter.

Discouragement

I HAVE BEEN READING BOOKS on writing for the past three days solid. I am a writer, have been a writer for thirty-five years, have myself written a book about writing, and I just decided to see what anyone else had to say. The books were fascinating to me, perhaps a little more naked to me than most books, since I was reading about something I know so well. I think I was looking for some new tricks to try to spruce up my own lagging spirits. What I learned is that I already know the tricks and I already practice them.

I do get up early and write in the morning (Dorothea Brande). I do take weekly excursions into the city, trying to see it with new eyes (Dorothea Brande). I do try to tell the truth (Brenda Ueland) and go for walks (Brenda Ueland) and include in my descriptions succulent detail (Natalie Goldberg). Doing all of this and still somehow falling flat brings me back to another rule: Write from where you actually are, not from where you wish you were.

Actually, I am sad. I am lurching through a tough season of overwork and underplay and I am not alive with excitement to much of anything. The world feels like a long wait at the post office, something to just be endured. How did this happen? What became of my sense of adventure? Why am I so discouraged? I think the answer comes back to work, work-related injuries that I have not let myself mourn.

Two months ago, I gave my musical *Avalon* over to be read. No one has read it yet. No one has called to say, "Good work. Keep going. Good for you." A month ago, I turned in a book to my publisher, and once again, no one has called to say, "Got the book. I am reading it. Good work!" Now, the adult part of me knows very well that my agent is busy and my publisher is busy and we all have better things to do than run around carefully patting each other on the back—but that is the adult part of me.

The part of me that creates is not adult. The part that makes musicals is about seven and is making up a song and wanting everyone to join in the game. The part of me that writes non-fiction creativity books may be about twelve and wanting all the other kids to try the experiments and see how they work for them. In short, I can act adult in my "career," but I had better be clear that why I have such a thing at all is because I am reasonably good at paying attention to the youngster in me that likes to make things.

It was the youngster in me who got discouraged and went to other writing books for a little company. It was the youngster in me who sniffed, "Oh, they use the same old tricks you do." It was the youngster in me who finally insisted that today's essay be about being sad and hurt and disappointed and to hell with whether or not such feelings were grown-up or warranted. There is always some bullying part of me that wants to say that my feelings don't matter and that I should just snap out of it! That's the part that just for today I am going to ignore.

When I let myself admit it, two months is a very long time to wait and see if someone liked the shiny Christmas present I bought for them. (Surely a musical is at least as special as a Christmas present.) When I let myself admit it, a month is a long time to wait and hear how the new book is received—after all, we all have a lot riding on how it goes, don't we? When I let myself admit it, being very mature is not a lot of fun, and it also may be asking my artist to turn into something that it shouldn't: a grown-up. I think my artist does much better at making things when it is a little childish and hot under the collar. I think my artist needs to find friends for its impulsive and quicksilver temperament, not try to cool it off into something more corporate and well considered.

DISCOURAGEMENT

Try this: What follows is a two-person task. You must select your confidant carefully and explain to him or her thoroughly his or her purpose. It is unmourned creative loss that turns into creative scar tissue. Our brainchildren deserve the dignity of a decent burial—and some of them have been known to come back to life when tendered such care.

Part One: Take pen in hand, number from 1 to 5, and list five creative wounds or disappointments. What has made you discouraged?

Part Two: Set a date with your creative confidant to go somewhere public yet private, a café, coffee shop, or restaurant. Once there, you will read out loud your list of creative injuries. Your confidant's job, quite simply, is to witness what you read. Do not be surprised if this exercise occasions some tears. Many of us have unmourned losses, and remembering them can cause an emotional thaw. Remember that once your energy has thawed, it is fluid again and available for your use. Sometimes our moistening tears help to resuscitate "dead" projects. Other times, we simply feel a sense of benevolent closure.

Cross-Country

THE TREES IN RIVERSIDE PARK are in full leaf. It is mid-May, and already the heat of the summer is promised. In just a few days, I will set out cross-country to Taos, New Mexico, where it is still snowing, although spring is fighting for a foothold. Once a full-time resident, now I live in Taos a third of the year. I catch late spring, full summer, and early fall.

The drive across country is a tricky business. I travel with my musical collaborator, Emma Lively, and our two small dogs, Tiger Lily and Charlotte, a long-tailed gold-and-white cocker spaniel and a small, sprightly Westie. The car is piled with suitcases of work, suitcases of clothes, and sheepskin throws to make beds for the dogs. We drive about five hundred miles a day, depending on our stamina, and then we must find lodging for the night that accepts dogs. We try to travel in the off-season, when motels have welcoming vacancies. Because it is difficult to predict exactly how far we can travel in a day, it is difficult to phone ahead for reservations. Then, too, there is the adventurous aspect of just striking out and seeing how far we can get.

The trip is a study in contrasts. We leave from New York's Riverside Drive with our doorman and superintendent helping and advising as we pack the car. We pull into a narrow dirt driveway and cross a rickety bridge when we get to Taos. There, the old adobe house stands empty, although a stray garter snake may be cooling itself in the shade of the porch. Last year, there was a shortage of food in the mountains, and the town of Taos was over-run by black bear mothers and their cubs. My property contains fruit trees and bushes filled with sour cherries. These make it a magnet for bears. Bessie Ortega, my eighty-three-year-old neigh-bor, reported sighting several. A friend of mine, a pianist, summers at a music school high in the mountains. There, at 10,000 feet, the bears are a routine and expected part of life.

It is a good adventure, driving across America twice a year. It divides the year into creative seasons. In Taos, we write and plan. The long days there lend themselves to prose and music. Nature aside, there's not too much cracking, and the lack of distraction pays off in terms of finished work. Back in New York, the sum-mer's work can be mounted and published. This year, we hope to finish a draft of a new book and a draft of an opera on Magellan. But that is once we get to Taos. In the meanwhile, there is the flurry of good-byes, the promise that we'll be back soon, in only four months.

CROSS-COUNTRY

Try this: Adventure is good for the soul. We know this, and yet we seldom allow our soul sufficient adventure. A weekly one-hour Artist Date, a solo, festive expedition undertaken just for ourselves, helps to restore our creative self. A longer and larger Artist Date, a real adventure, brings to the soul a sense of joy and well-being. Take pen in hand. Number from 1 to 10. Finish the following phrase as rapidly as possible:

1. *A great adventure I'd love to have is*
   _____.

2. *A great adventure I'd love to have is*
   _____.

3. *A great adventure I'd love to have is*
   _____.

4. *A great adventure I'd love to have is*
   _____.

5. *A great adventure I'd love to have is*
   _____.

6. *A great adventure I'd love to have is*
   _____.

7. *A great adventure I'd love to have is*

   _____.

8. *A great adventure I'd love to have is*

   _____.

9. *A great adventure I'd love to have is*

   _____.

10. *A great adventure I'd love to have is*

    _____.

Scan your list. Select the adventure that sounds the most delectable to you. Devise one small step you can take toward having that adventure. Take that step.

Finding Our Feet

IN ORDER TO BEGIN, we must start with where we are. That precise point is the taking-off place, the entryway to where we are trying to go. It is a morning in mid-May. I have just driven across the country from New York to New Mexico. I arrived "home" in Taos yesterday; my familiar house feels like a foreign country, and I do not know how to unfurl my days here. The sky outside my writing room window is blue. Deeper blue mountains bulk in the distance. Closer in, the sun beats down on the tin roof of my old adobe house and the day stretches out with languor. That is where I am. Where are you?

Often, we are dissatisfied with where we are. We want to be somewhere else, somewhere more finished and respectable before we begin. "Let me just get my legs under me," we think. "Then I will think about the art I want to make."

The truth is, thinking about the art we want to make is part of how we get our legs underneath us. When we start with where we are, however awkward and unfinished, we start with something real. The something real may be "Stop, Julia, I don't feel ready!" but that is as good a place to begin as any—and so we start. We take our pen to the page and we move our hand across it, listening to the faint, whispery sound of paper: Here we go, here we are, ready, aim, and fire. It is not so bad, really, writing from where we are instead of from some imaginary place. It is good, really, to start with the truth: "Today I am frightened. My life stretches in front of me like a highway going nowhere that I know. I slip into the car. I put the car in gear. I touch the gas. My God, I am going somewhere, but where?"

When we say we are afraid to begin a project, we are actually saying something else: "I am afraid of how I will feel as I continue." We do not want to start because we do not know that we can continue. It is not the start, it is the finish that troubles us.

Wanting to know where we are going is often how we fail to go anywhere at all. Rather than surrender to the mystery of the creative journey, we want to know each sight we will see, each obstacle we will confront. Each "something" that we will encounter if we dare to begin.

The truth is that we cannot know where our creative trail is taking us. We cannot predict precisely who and what it is we will become. The only certainty is that we will change from who and what we are. We will become something larger and something more, but exactly the form that something more and larger will take is a creation that we have not yet created and cannot demand to know.

"Lord, I believe. Help my unbelief" is an excellent prayer for travelers, and as creative beings, travelers are what we are at the core. The refusal to begin our journey doesn't keep us from having one. We do our days in motion anyway, like prisoners making their daily rounds within the walls. It is when we willingly embark, praying, "Take me where you would have me go; make me what you would have me be," that our journey becomes at once God's and more uniquely our own.

Each of us is unique and irreplaceable. There is only one of us in all of time. We are on this earth, partnered always by unseen forces that would guide us and guard us as we journey into the unknown. No one else can take our journey for us. Two people setting off side by side will still encounter different sights, different wonders. The openness to begin is all the openness we are required to have each day. We start today, and tomorrow we start again, and the day after we start again, as we will the day after that. In this way, and no other, does our journey come to us. We begin. The rest unfolds through us.

FINDING OUR FEET

Try this: Think of what you are about to do as a field report to yourself. Take pen in hand and describe precisely where you are and how you feel about it. Nothing is too petty to be included. Allow yourself to gripe on the page. You are sending out an SOS and giving your exact coordinates. Every detail you include helps the rescue squad to know what's needed. Be precise. Where are you at?

Drought

I AM BACK IN my little crimson writing room in New Mexico. My desk looks west, over the tin roof of the adobe next door, toward a distant mountain range. A large willow tree lashes in the wind. It is very dry. The wind is stiff and full of dust. We need rain.

One of the critical issues in any creative life is how to survive the periods of drought, those long patches where ideas feel few and far between and when our creative spirit feels parched for lack of moisture. Droughts stretch too long, and we always feel they are endless. We find it hard to take our cue from the natural world, knowing that rain will come again, ideas will once more flow freely.

When I am in a period of drought, my chief enemy is despair. I am afraid to harbor hope, and yet it is the gentle harboring of hope that is the antidote to dryness of the spirit. In arid times we must practice a very gentle discipline. We must keep on keeping on. Morning Pages are never more important than in those periods when we seem to eke them onto the page a drop at a time. The slightest trickle, the merest hint of water, creative juice, is what we are after.

Yesterday, driving into town, the wind was so stiff that the car rocked, swayed by its fierce bouts. Dust blew in great rust-colored clouds. Grit filled the air. I had been eight months in the verdant East, dripping with moisture and green. I had heard, but only heard, that "we were dry this year," at home in Taos, but it took seeing to be believed.

My aging neighbor stepped out to greet me as I pulled the car into the drive. She waved a hand at the parched earth. "Papa brings the water in a bucket," she said. "At night there sometimes isn't any water."

At eighty-three, my neighbor has been through drought before. She knows that it will pass, and she shares that knowledge along with her advice on what to do in the meantime: "Wash and bathe early in the day. Try not to use much water. There isn't much to use."

When we are in a period of creative drought, we must believe that we carry our own water, that we can gently tap the inner stream if we are kind with ourselves, and patient. The grace of creativity is a great underground river. It flows on, untouched by the events and the apparent droughts of our outer life. Like the great rivers that flow within the earth, it is there, waiting for us to acknowledge it and dip into it with humility.

Most droughts of the spirit occur because we have tried to be too self-sufficient. We have forgotten that our creativity is a spiritual gift with its taproot in Spirit and not in our own will. "Not I, but the father doeth the works," Christ told us. Great artists through the ages have insisted that they were merely channels for divine energy, that God worked through them, bringing their art to form. We hear testimony to this fact from Brahms, from Puccini, from Blake. When we remember that our position as artists is a humble one, we begin to feel the gentle flow. When we start to listen to what would be born through us instead of trying to force into being a "something" that we will, then we begin to write or paint or sculpt or dance more freely. Feeling our connection to the divine, we feel less alone, less the sole architect of what it is we would accomplish.

Does this mean that an artist is empty and without ambition? I don't think so. I think it means that our ambitions must be surrendered to a higher force for proper fulfillment. "This is what I have in mind, help me" is a worthy artist's prayer.

When I was first getting sober and learning the ideas of art as a spiritual practice, I was told to post a little sign in my writing area: "Dear God, I will take care of the quantity. You take care of the quality." This notion ran counter to all my ego-driven ideas about art and authorship. It shrank the artistic job to a very simple one: Show up and try to write whatever seemed to want to be written.

In the long years since those early lessons, I have learned that the lessons are sound and that my relationship to my creativity, in order to stay healthy, must remain one of openness and receptivity. I must strive not to be "full of ideas" but instead to be empty of self-will so that my ideas might come into me more easily.

Creative droughts do not end through willfulness. They end through the act of surrender. They end through the prayer "Show me what you would have me do." Our creative condition is grounded in and subject to our spiritual condition. We may daily strive to "work" but we will get further if we daily strive to "serve." It is not that God's will and ours are at opposite ends of the table but, rather, that we can seat ourselves near God or far from God, at the right hand or at a remove. God is the Great Creator. The Great Creator takes delight in us and our creations. Inviting this larger creative spirit to participate in our work is acknowledging the right order of things. We have been "made," and we in turn are intended to "make things." How much better we do this when we seek our creator's help.

DROUGHT

Try this: In any period of creative drought, kindness is critical. We must become for ourselves the good mother, gentling the turbulent or despairing heart. Some of us do not know where to begin with kindness. What follows is a list of ten possibilities. Read them, then find ten of your own from which to choose.

1. *Buy bath salts and oils*
2. *Buy fresh berries*
3. *Drink more herbal tea*
4. *Get a manicure*
5. *Schedule a massage*
6. *Go to bed an hour early every night for a week*
7. *Take a walk*
8. *Buy a good new pen*
9. *Do the mending*
10. *Have my hair professionally conditioned*

Choosing any of these from either my list or yours will be a step in the direction of kindness and self-nurturing.

Drama

A TREMENDOUS WIND sweeps down from the mountains. It carries both dust and debris. On the porch, a pigeon shelters against the wind, moving the dogs to mayhem in their frantic barking. The pine trees whip sideways. The willow tree lashes the earth. The air is fresh with change and heady with ozone. This weather is dramatic.

There are two uses for drama. We can use it to distract ourselves from work or we can use it to fuel our work. Drama contains energy, and that energy can be tapped. The cottonwoods along the creek rustle in the wind and shake loose great clouds of snowy fluff. The fluff floats in the air, coming softly to settle on a window ledge. That fluff reminds me of inspiration—sometimes so soft and gentle that it is easy not to notice it. It is particularly easy to ignore inspiration if we are in the midst of drama.

It is one of the many false myths about creativity that artists thrive on dramatic lives. The truth may be the opposite, that our creative lives are dramatic enough and that we thrive on everyday lives that are dull, routine, and structured. Artists need structure, and many times we must devise it for ourselves, setting up work schedules and deadlines in lives that are too wide open to be productive.

"I crave structure," says writer Natalie Goldberg, who begins her day by sitting *zazen,* then progresses to a writing session, a painting session, and a long daily walk.

My day is structured similarly. I begin with Morning Pages, followed by guided writing, followed by music, followed by writing, followed by walking. When I can fit it in, I also do piano time, and I wish for days twice their length so that I could grid in more activities.

In the midst of personal drama, it can be harder to hold to our creative grid. We may be tempted to binge on phone time or lengthy heartfelt conversations across the kitchen table over cups of tea. Drama is seductive, and artists must learn to not be readily seduced. Our work time must be sacrosanct, and if it isn't, drama soon seeps into our personalities. We feel ill tempered and out of sorts. The world goes off-kilter and it tends to stay there until we get back to working.

The domestic partners of working artists must learn to live with the rhythm of creative work. An untimely interruption can wreak havoc on a day's productivity. We want to be like regular people, but we are not. The thread of thought that we are listening to may not be easy to recapture—and so we must take care.

It is not that artists are precious. We are actually hardy and often user-friendly as long as the simplest boundaries are in place. Many writers and painters learn to turn off their phones, leaving a cheery message that announces they will be glad to talk—"after work." Studios and writing spaces are off-limits for the casual visitor. Drop-ins are not really welcome, although sometimes when one occurs we fall on it like a ravenous dog, glad to be distracted. But it is the lack of distraction that really serves us, the long hours of boredom that we are left to fill with our own devices.

I live two thirds of the year in busy Manhattan and one third of the year in sleepy Taos. In Taos, I tend to get great swaths of writing done, as there is little to distract me. The drive into town is a drive. It is all too apparent that I really am abandoning my work if I get in the car, and so I tend to put off "town" until late in the day, after the music and the prose have had their time.

There is something very productive about having days that unfurl with cookie-cutter sameness, leaving the drama where it belongs—in the work itself. Many artists find that the drama in their own temperaments also grows curbed as their creative work progresses. A taste for crazy lovers may be replaced by a steady relationship. A fondness for alcohol may give way to sobriety in the name of productivity. Over time, drama tends to be outgrown and left behind. There is drama enough in the work itself, in the doing of it or the not doing of it—and the not doing of it becomes so painfully dramatic that we tend to avoid that too.

The wind is still whipping down the mountain. The heads of trees still bob and dance. This essay has been written despite the temptation to stand, nose pressed to the window, staring out at the great and showy storm. Instead, the storm has become a part of the work. The work has grown large enough to hold its tumult, and the gentle pages of this book on creative process have continued to build up. This is the best use of drama.

DRAMA

Try this: For most of us, drama is a sip of creative poison. Once we get into a drama, we lose focus on our creative jumps and focus on the drama instead. Because of this, we must monitor our life for trouble spots: dramas that we could become entangled in. Take pen in hand. Number from 1 to 5. Scan your life for potential areas of drama. For example:

1. *Tony's gossiping about me*
2. *Jim's lack of loyalty*
3. *My financial insecurity*
4. *My sister's difficult divorce*
5. *My battle with overweight*

Scanning your list, choose one dramatic situation as a booster rocket to fuel your art. Holding the situation lightly in mind, move directly into your art. Whenever your energies flag, remind yourself again of your dramatic situation and create art straight at it. You are practicing the discipline of *non illegitimi te carborundum*:

Don't let the bastards get you down.

Taming Time

ONCE AGAIN, the hot, dry westerly winds are blowing through. Along the highways, hundred-foot-high dust devils spin the hazy air. The heat and the drought create illusion: Time itself seems to be cooking in the hot summer air.

Time is a primary concern in dealing with creative block. Most of us think, "If only I had more time, then I would work." We have a fantasy that there is such a thing as good creative time, an idyll of endless, seamless time unfolding invitingly for us to frolic in creatively. No such bolts of limitless time exist for most of us. Our days are chopped into segments, and if we are to be creative, we must learn to use the limited time we have.

When ego is siphoned off creativity, when creativity becomes one more thing we do, like the laundry, then it takes far less time to do it. Much of our desire for creative time has to do with our trying to coax ourselves into being in the right mood to create. We want to "feel like it," and when we don't, or don't quickly, we think the solution is more time. Actually, the solution is less attention to the vagaries of mood. In short, creativity needs to become daily, doable, and nonnegotiable, something as quotidian as breathing.

When we make a special occasion out of our art, we rob ourselves of the time we actually have. When we make a ceremony out of the right paper, the right noise level, the right pen and precise circumstance, we are actually creating many false conditions that make our art not more possible but more impossible. "I can't think when it's noisy" or "when the kids are home" or "when the phone's going off." We may not like thinking under those conditions, but we can think under them and we owe it to ourselves to learn that we can. By making our creativity nonnegotiable, we do it a little every day no matter what our mood and no matter what our judgment of the work. What we are after is the gut-level knowledge that our creativity is both doable and portable. We can work no matter how "adverse" the conditions. If we are writers, we can write waiting at the doctor's office. If we are visual artists, we can sketch there.

The less precious we are about how and when we do our work, the more precious it can be to us. We are like parents who take their infant everywhere. The child learns to thrive in many environments, and so, too, can our brainchild, art.

It is one of the ironies of the sabbatical system that very often the year free to work becomes a year free from work as a large and unbearable block rears its head—a block invited by the large swath of time earmarked "Now, work!" Creativity is something like an athletic career. We start with walking, move to gentle jogging, advance from there to short races and from there to longer races before undertaking a marathon. So, too, in our creative mileage we need to build our stamina. We need to exercise our creative muscles daily in the small windows of time available to us. We might want to think of it as the creative equivalent of an aerobics workout—twenty minutes will do in a pinch, forty minutes is nice, and once a week it is a pleasure to get in a long and leisurely run.

When we think about our creativity in terms of training, we begin to understand the importance of working despite our moods. Just as a determined and devoted runner runs despite the weather, we need to learn to weather our moods and work on our stormy days as well as those when we are in a sunny mood. Putting in our daily jot of time at a typewriter or at the easel teaches us that we can produce when we don't feel like it, when our censor is shrieking that what we are doing is no good and of no earthly good to anyone.

If we wait for the time when we have our inner censor's approval, that imaginary time when it bows gracefully and says, "Yes, you're a wonderful artist, go to it," we may wait a very long time indeed; in fact, we may wait our entire career for such a green light. In my experience, red flashing lights are what the censor loves to issue. That, and dire warnings: "This book is terrible. Don't write it" is what my censor has said to me over what, in clear-eyed retrospect, turned out to be some of my better work.

And yet, time itself is not the issue it appears to be. In order to use our time freely, in order to grab at the small windows of time we have available, we must train our inner censor to stand aside and allow us to work. The training of the censor, the *taming* of the censor, is one of the primary accomplishments of Morning Pages. Each day as we take to the page, our censor weighs in with opinions. "Oh, you are so negative, so ungrateful, such a spiritual midget," the censor opines as we lay our life onto the page. We learn to keep writing. We learn to tame time. We learn to write through the censor's critiques. We learn to say, "Thank you for sharing," and keep right on moving. In short, we do not kill our censor off, but we learn to evade it. We learn to live and to work while ignoring its steady stream of negatives. This saves us a lot of time. We do not pause to argue with our censor when we are writing Morning Pages. We simply move straight onto the page. This is a portable, transferable skill. We learn not to stop and engage with the censor, that great time waster, to and move straight ahead into our work.

The inner censor doesn't really want us to work. It wants us to spend all of our time dealing with it. It is like a greedy lover who has a penchant for staging dramas. There will never be enough drama to satisfy the censor. It has an incurable, insatiable appetite for drama, and this is why as you progress in your work, it will progress in its nastiness. Let us say you have written a fine first novel. The censor now cannot use its old line "You are an amateur author." Now that you are published, it must come up with something more sinister, and so it says, "You are a one-book author." If we bother to engage in a debate over this, we are exactly where the censor wants us: wasting our precious work time over a block. This is what so many therapists fail to realize. They think that focusing on the block will dissolve it. Actually, focusing on a block simply enlarges it. Blocks are an everyday part of the artist's life, and they range from the scary to the very scary. No one is immune to them, and those who claim they are are just whistling in the dark. The trick with a block is to accept the fact that it is there and to work anyway. This is best done by working in small doses, slipping work past the nose of the guardian gargoyle. "Just a little sketching," just divert its attention and accomplish what we can.

There are any number of excellent tricks for doing this, and chief among them is the simple lie. We tell the censor, "What I am doing right now doesn't count. It's just a rough draft." The censor allows rough drafts because it thinks it will get its perfectionist innings in later—and many a rough draft holds up surprisingly well and a further draft can be designated "still rough," and so on through repeated drafts or sketches while the censor stands to one side, waiting for its chance to slay us—which keeps being gently postponed.

The habit of daily work lulls the censor. Daily work is so much like Morning Pages that the censor lapses into torpor. It knows very well that pages can be accomplished despite its best attempts to the contrary. If we work daily and with the same studied non-chalance, the censor begins to be convinced that it can't really stop us and so it will curl up, snoring loudly, and make a show of indifference to our efforts—which is exactly what we want it to do.

At bottom, the censor is a lot like the hundred-foot-high dust devils dancing during a drought. It looks dangerous. It acts dangerous. But it is not dangerous. As we learn to think of our censor's attacks as time-wasting diversions, mere dust devils, we begin to claim for ourselves the amounts of time we do have—and that is often far more time than we have previously acknowledged.

Try this: Most of us procrastinate when it comes to time. We tell ourselves we "don't have enough time to do X," an activity or undertaking that frightens us. The truth is that it is not our lack of time that is the issue, it is our lack of courage. Take pen in hand and number from 1 to 5. List five tasks you've been procrastinating about, telling yourself you had "no time." Here are some examples:

1. *Rereading my play*
2. *Cleaning up my work area*
3. *Sorting through my financial papers*
4. *Doing my laundry*
5. *Writing a letter to Bob*

Take time in your own hands now, and choose one task from your list to execute. Within a week, try to execute your whole list, proving to yourself that you *do* have time.

Trust

OUTSIDE MY STUDY WINDOW, two white Arabians and a bay graze peacefully. They are not troubled by the day's length, their bolt of time and how to fill it. For them it is a simple matter of appetite and trust. They will reach for mouthful after mouthful of what they want and need, and the sun will rise in the sky, arc across it, and set in the west without any further effort on their part.

Many times, when we are in doubt of our creative trajectory, it is because we are lacking in trust. We do not trust that a peaceful unfolding awaits our appetites. We are afraid to reach for what we want, afraid that as we reach, what we hunger for will be snatched from us. We believe in a capricious and withholding God.

In times of doubt or trouble, it is worthwhile to try out this phrase: "If everything were in divine order, then I could gently expect _____." We might find that we could expect time enough or support enough to finish our project. We might find that we could expect a financial flow sufficient to our needs. The "what we could expect" might surprise us, identifying some previously unacknowledged want: company enough, perhaps, when we had not known we were lonely.

Late in his long and illustrious career, Joseph Campbell remarked that in every life could be seen the tracery of destiny. He believed that as we aged, we could begin to trace the patterns in our own life, begin to sense when we were unfolding properly and when we were trying to force a direction that ran counter to our intended path.

I believe we can encounter the tracery that Campbell speaks of, but I believe that many of us are fearful, and we expect to encounter "no" where we might just as easily find "yes." Our imaginations, both active and causal, tend toward the negative. Impending doom looms on our creative horizon but seldom visits. And yet there is a strain in the prolonged wince that we often endure as we brace ourselves for the worst. We do this from a habit of doubt and strain. In times of doubt and strain, there is another phrase worth using: "I am grounded in my spiritual purpose; there are no emergencies."

Most of us live with a continual sense of emergency. We have a fear that we are too late and not enough to wrestle a happy destiny from the hands of the gods. What if there is no emergency? What if there is no need to wrestle? What if our only need is receptivity, a gentle openness to guidance? What if, like the Arabian horses grazing outside my window, we are able to simply trust?

When we trust ourselves, we become both more humble and more daring. When we trust ourselves, we move surely. There is no unnecessary strain in our grasp as we reach out to meet life. There is no snatching at people and events, trying to force them to give us what we think we want. We become what we are meant to be. It is that simple. We become what we are, and we do it by being who we are, not who we strive to be.

We are right-sized. We are who and what we are meant to be. All that we need, all that we require, is coming toward us. We need only meet life, not combat it. We need only encounter each day's questions, not raise a fist at the heavens over the questions of tomorrow.

"Just relax" is not advice that most of us respond to easily. We do better with a more active phrase: Focus on the now. In the precise now, no matter how painful our life events, we are always all right. What may be hard is always bearable—not perhaps in our projected future, but there, in that moment, precisely now.

The horses outside my study window live in the now. They meet life with the gentle expectancy that as they move their velvet muzzles across the green earth, they will be fed and life will be good. For most of us, a similar faith—I will be fed; life will be good—feels radical. And yet we are creatures made by the Great Creator and shaped exactly as it would have us. What is there to fix? What is there to be punished for? We are as we were intended to be.

TRUST

Try this: It has been said that faith is theoretical, while trust is grounded in our actual experience. Take pen in hand and list five situations you do not trust to work out. For example:

1. *Finding a new apartment*
2. *Doing a successful rewrite*
3. *Healing the rift in my friendship with Doris*
4. *Finding the right form for my relationship with Ted*
5. *Finding a new job I actually like*

Take pen in hand again. Now list five situations that have *already* worked out despite your lack of trust. For example:

1. *Fixing Act II of my play*
2. *Finding a piano I could afford*
3. *Finding a successful diet*
4. *Negotiating my contract*
5. *Finding proper day care*

Good Husbandry

A SCORCHING WESTERLY WIND again blows through the cottonwoods. The underbellies of the leaves flash silver. Even with the haze of dust-filled air created by drought, New Mexico is a miracle of changing light. Stands of Russian olives flash bright as dimes; the sage, too, is silvery. Although one of the poorest states, New Mexico is the colors of money—silver, gold, and green sprouting from the copper earth.

Seeking to end a creative drought, we must tap our inner well. We do so by fighting depression and tapping into our capacity for attention. A drive along a dusty highway becomes an exercise not in sameness but in differences. A dust devil dances on the horizon. The blacktop road shimmers in the heat. Cattle graze hopefully on dry and brittle grasses. It is a good sign the grasses are yet here. For days now, the afternoon air has taunted the senses with a hint of rain. Like a fickle lover, the clouds promise to come across, and then they don't. Creeks and riverbeds are arid vessels, holding the scantiest trickle where torrents like to flow. The acequia are dry. There is no water to irrigate. The older Spanish people take buckets and clamber down the creek beds for water for their gardens. Food is grown here, in the Hispanic community, not bought, and the lack of water translates to a lack of food. No one waters at midday. It wastes the water and burns the plants. Only at twilight do the gardeners emerge, cool as shadows, sloshing their buckets. They give each plant just enough, and with their careful husbandry the gardens still thrive, rich with zucchini and rhubarb. The apple and apricot crops this year will be lean, impacted by the drought.

When we give our lives the gift of attention, our consciousness blossoms. Attention is an act of love, an act of connection. Like a child in a good home, our art responds to a nurturing atmosphere. Ideas nudge their way toward the fore. It is as if we are being trusted with new insights, trusted because we have shown our capacity for attention. The daily writing of Morning Pages takes attention. So, too, does the practice of Walks. Just up the road from my old adobe house there grazes a herd of buffalo—shaggy and stub-legged. Walk a little farther, and you meet the llamas, like doe-eyed, furry camels. Of course, not all Walks feature such exotic denizens, but all Walks do feature insights. We use the phrase "body of knowledge," and that phrase is quite literal. Our body has knowledge to give us—that, and inspiration.

Writer and teacher Brenda Ueland tells us: "I'll tell you what works for me, and you must do it alone and every day: a long, five- or six-mile walk." Such good advice notwithstanding, most of us can't indulge in such a long daily ramble. But we can walk a little, and when we do, the rewards are immediate.

"Julia, I thought I had no ideas, that I was completely burned out. But then I started walking and the ideas started coming again," I am often told. A few crowded city blocks can still yield the cat in the window box or the lovely cornice above a door. The quality of light shifts dramatically from neighborhood to neighborhood in Manhattan. The city is an island, and with focused attention one can note the fog-wrapped western shore touching the Hudson. All environments are earmarked by minute markers, special and specific. Our focused attention brings us a wealth of experience, and that, too, is a literal phrase. We become rich with images and impressions, fine distinctions that confer distinctions on our art. It has been remarked that genius is largely a matter of energy. It is certainly true that great artists are characterized by great energy— a vibrancy we can cultivate by engaging fully from moment to moment. Great writers, like the Brontës, inhabited ordinary and limited lives. What was unlimited was the quality of attention they brought to bear on their experience. We, too, can bring attention to the fore of our lives. Oscar Hammerstein remarked, "A hundred million miracles are happening every day." He is right.

Try this: Most of us have many small areas in which we fail to husband ourselves. We see a problem, but we neglect to address it. We procrastinate about self-care, telling ourselves that we will get to it once our creative project is finished. The truth is that a little self-care can make finishing our creative projects much easier. This exercise is called Filling in the Form. Its benefit is a sense of well-being. Take pen in hand. List three tiny, benevolent changes you could make in the following areas:

1. *Your bathroom*
    1.
    2.
    3.
2. *Your bedroom*
    1.
    2.
    3.
3. *Your living room*
    1.
    2.
    3.

4. *Your kitchen*

    1.

    2.

    3.

5. *Your car*

    1.

    2.

    3.

6. *Wardrobe from shoulders to top of the head*

    1.

    2.

    3.

7. *Wardrobe from shoulders to waist*

    1.

    2.

    3.

8. *Wardrobe from waist to knees*

    1.

    2.

    3.

9. *Wardrobe from knees to floor*

    1.

    2.

    3.

10. *Tools you use for your art*
    1.
    2.
    3.

Filling in the Form is a deceptively simple yet powerful exercise in self-worth. Execute one tiny change from each category.

Getting at It

ONE OF THE MOST effective ways we sabotage ourselves from a life in the arts is by waiting for that imaginary day when "it" will be "easier." We think of going to the page or to the easel, and then we think, "It's too hard. If I wait a little, it won't be so hard."

Waiting for art to be easy, we make it hard. We take our emotional temperature and find ourselves below normal, lacking in resolve. We would do it, we know we could do it, but we decide to wait until the doing of it is more effortless. In other words, we put ourselves in a passive position relative to our art. We want something outside of ourselves, the wind of inspiration, to blow our way and then we will get at it.

The truth is that getting at it is what makes getting at it easier. Each day that we write creates a habit of writing in us. Each day we go to the barre and do our pliés creates an inner as well as outer flexibility that makes dancing easier. It is the easier and softer way to work today, if only for a few minutes, no matter how hard or impossible it seems. Each inch we inch forward is a tiny little notch in our self-esteem: Yes, I did do it.

Most of us want not only to do it but to do it well. We want not just to write but to write brilliantly, not just to paint but to paint a masterwork. Our inner perfectionist has standards that we stumble against. Our inner perfectionist takes each stumble to reinforce cruelly, "What kind of artist are you, falling short that way?"

Many very fine artists fall short of their inner perfectionist daily. The trick is "daily." They fall short and then the next day they fall short again. Over time, the accumulated falling-shorts add up to some estimable progress—you would barely know they had fallen short.

Yesterday I had a visit from a young artist. Quick, bright, talented, and funny, he was in a slough of despond. And why? He was waiting for it to get easier. He had moved from Los Angeles to Taos, telling himself that he would write more in Taos. Now he was in Taos, and he wasn't writing. He felt lazy, angry, disappointed in himself. His inner perfectionist was loaded with ammunition about how worthless he was, what a bad artist he was, what a shallow and ineffective person he was. What could he do in the face of this daily inner barrage?

I suggested that he begin at the beginning with Morning Pages. They can't be done well. They can't be done poorly. They are either done or not done—no matter what the inner perfectionist says. "Just start tomorrow," I urged the young artist. "Simply get up and write, 'This is how I feel.'"

When we are not working, it is not because we are lazy. It is because we are frightened. We have bought into the idea that in order to work we must be able to work "well," and we are afraid of working poorly.

"I am willing to work poorly" is often a very good place to start. By surrendering our grandiose expectations, we come down to size. Being willing to work poorly, we may actually work very well. Some of the best work is done on the worst days. Some of the finest ideas lie at the very bottom of the well.

When we are willing to scoop the well bottom, our inner perfectionist backs off a little. If there is one thing that the inner perfectionist cannot battle, it is humility. Think about it for a moment. Doesn't the inner perfectionist always hook you in the ego? "You're not going to be any good," the inner perfectionist spits out.

When we respond, "That's okay. I think I will try it anyhow," the inner perfectionist comes up fresh out of stratagems. There's no fighting humility. Humility carries the day.

Today was a day when I lay in bed, mere feet from my typewriter, and thought, "I'd like it to be easier." Fortunately, I am an experienced writer and I heard the demonic little voice for what it was. My inner perfectionist wanted me not to work today. I have been working a lot lately, which is good for my self-esteem, and the inner perfectionist just hates that. I knew that sabotage was afoot, and so I wrote.

I believe we are creations of the Great Creator and that we are intended to be creative ourselves. I believe that when we humbly cooperate by making something every day, we are making something also out of ourselves, and it is a something that God intends for us—souls joyous and effective, active and self-actualized. I do not think it is pushing things too far to wonder if the hiss of the inner perfectionist isn't in fact somewhat satanic, the undoing of our good and our good nature.

It is my hope that the young artist who came to visit yesterday got to the page today. It is so easy, from my perspective, to see the criminal waste that comes from listening to the inner perfectionist who urges us to wait until we can do something perfectly, and with ease, before we can do something at all. "Be gone, Satan!" we should snap, setting ourselves gently to the work, knowing that it is the doing of work that makes work easier, the simple doing of work no matter how hard it may feel to begin.

GETTING AT IT

Try this: Most of us accomplish far more in a day than we give ourselves credit for. Focused on what we haven't yet done, we ignore what we have. Almost any day is earmarked by small accomplishments that move us closer to our larger goals. Take pen in hand and number from 1 to 5. List five ways in which you have inched forward.

1. *Did my Morning Pages*
2. *Took a Walk at lunch hour*
3. *Stayed on my diet*
4. *Called to check on my sister*
5. *Paid my bills*

As a quick scan of your list will show, small ordinary actions can pay off in terms of our self-worth. We do not need to do something large or heroic in order to feel better about ourselves. Small, gentle daily actions do add up.

Keeping Safe

THERE IS AN INEXORABLE, desiccating wind blowing in from the west. It is laden with red dust, and a walk outside means a quick trip to the shower afterward. We are in a season of heavy drought, and the wind underscores and exacerbates the parched earth. Like the famed, murderous Santa Anas that sweep down from the Hollywood Hills, these winds are seasonal, and veterans of living in New Mexico speak of them with respect. "The terrible winds are here. Be careful."

As prissy as it may sound, "Be careful" is useful creative advice. It means to be gently thoughtful of yourself and your progress, not to expect too much or, on the other hand, to require too little. "Keep on keeping on" is what the sages say, and it is well-earned advice.

It is easy, in times of a creative drought, when the going is tough and seems fruitless, to engage in outsize drama. "It will always be like this," our fears say. The truth is that droughts pass and one day the terrible wind does not visit again. The truth is that if we can avoid drama, we are better off. But how do we avoid drama when drama is all around us? Many of us live and work in dramatic, high-stress environments. We do not so much avoid drama as endure it. With experience, we learn to set a governor on the level of drama we will tolerate. This governor keeps our creative engine from over-revving.

The first defense against drama is a schedule, a regular routine that is hewed to, easy days or hard. For me that schedule begins with Morning Pages. It includes a spate of steadying phone calls to my far-flung beloveds, and then it requires that I sit at the type-writer, press fingers to the keys, and march forward a little on the writing project of the moment. For my sister, Libby, a painter, her schedule demands easel time, time spent in her studio, at her work space, even if it is time spent preparing to work more than really working. For my friend Thea, a dancer, her schedule requires a daily workout, an homage to the importance of sheer fitness in the art she makes but is not always making. My friend Jackie, an actress, prepares new monologues and scenes. All of us have learned to work when we are not officially working. The regular-ity of a schedule goes a long way toward overturning the great artist's fear: I will never work again.

The second defense against drama is familiarity. It helps to schedule not only a regular regime of work but also a regular ret-inue of people. We are creatures who require companionship, and that is true even in pursuit of our art. I have learned to make what in 12-step work they call "sandwich calls." I pick up the phone, call a friend, and say, "I am about to work on my project." Then I get off the phone, work on the project, and when I have finished, I call back, making the sandwich: "I did just work. Thank you for being there."

There are people who feel that artists should be beyond such baby steps. I am not so sure about that. I have known many estimable artists. Some of the most celebrated have learned to treat their artistic process with the gentlest and yet most regimented care. A director I know posts a schedule with his office indicating just when he will be working on what project. The schedule reinforces the fact that when two o'clock comes he will retreat to the editing room and that when five o'clock comes he will meet for a writing session on a new project. By scheduling his time and by naming the endeavor he will undertake in each slot, he imitates a schoolboy's schedule—English in second period, math in third, lunch break in fourth, biology in fifth, etc. The set schedule with its predetermined jumps also makes the artist a promise that there will be no exhausting bingeing in any one arena. In this regard, the modus operandi is "easy does it." The threat of dramatic deadlines is kept at bay because work is being done daily, a little at a time.

For many an artist, the best tool that he or she can muster is something called a "grid." A grid is a schedule of blocked-out time in which daily expectations are met. My grid, for example, contains time for Morning Pages, time for phone calls to friends and family, time for daily writing, and time for daily music. Additionally, as a sober alcoholic, I grid in time to keep my sobriety intact as a priority. If I meet my grid on any given day, I am guaranteed a productive day and my odds are better at having a nondramatic day.

Why all this talk about the danger of drama? It is because personal drama is the enemy of art. When our time is spent on high-stakes conflict, it is not spent on art. When our time is siphoned off into too many needy phone calls or too much hand-holding, then our imagination becomes engaged not in the making of art but in the making of peace. The phrase "peace at any cost" is telling, and often the price that we are paying is the making of our art.

With a grid in place and expectations of productivity laid out in black and white, it becomes easy to see how the emotional bender can cost us work time. High drama is high-ticket behavior for most people but especially for artists.

Caroline, an actress, has a long investment both in her career and in a turbulent relationship. It is difficult to work on a monologue if last night's dramatic dialogue is still being played in her head.

"I just wish I had the same feelings for you that I have for her," Caroline's straying partner confronted her.

Caroline, actively seeking to avoid drama, listened but did not pick up the bait.

"I really have to work on my scene," she told her dramatic lover and, with that, poured all of her turbulent emotions into preparing Lady Macbeth.

"I knew I had a choice," Caroline says. "I knew I could use all of my energy going, 'Love me, love me' or I could do something that would make *me* feel more lovable. I chose to work on my work."

Most of us are lucky enough not to have Caroline's level of daily drama, but most of us know exactly where we can drum up some drama when we want to. Concerned about our friends' well-being, we can focus obsessively on their affairs. Alternatively, we can grid in friendship time and keep it largely confined to the block provided for it. This isn't heartless. Our friends are still close at hand, just not so close that they smother our working hours with their unconscious demands.

When the heavy, hot winds are blowing, veteran New Mexicans keep their doors and windows shut. Let the wind howl outside the house. Don't give it entry. In the same way, when the hot, dry winds of a creative drought seem to threaten us with extinc-

· *129* ·

tion, we can make our creative house snug and serene. We can make a grid and stick to it gently. We can forge ahead, however modestly. We can remember that the phrase "easy does it" doesn't mean just "oh, calm down." It also means "easy accomplishes it," and the "it" we are aiming to accomplish is the making of art in an artful life.

KEEPING SAFE

Try this: In order to feel safety, most of us require that our lives contain continuity and structure. Many modern lives do not automatically contain these things. We must work to put continuity and structure in place. Take pen in hand and plan five ways in which you can increase your sense of safety by increasing your commitment to continuity and structure. For example:

1. *Do Morning Pages*
2. *Call your sister back home once weekly*
3. *Send regular e-mails to your close friends*
4. *Select a buddy to check in with daily for anything you find hard*
5. *Attend church, a 12-step group, or hobby club regularly*

Just Do It

WILDFIRES RAGE in Arizona and Colorado. New Mexico, pincered in between, is blanketed in smoke. The 13,000-foot Sangre de Cristo Mountains are erased; they simply cannot be seen behind the wall of smoke. There are advisory warnings posted for those with respiratory ailments. For everyone, eyes sting and tempers flare. As long as the smoke persists, so will a heightened irritability. Smoke and irritability go together. Simple as that.

For most artists, not working and irritability go together. There is nothing that medicates a certain kind of unease like working does. Cheerful self-chat—"You're a worthy person whether you are working or not"—does nothing to lighten its burden. No, when an artist is not working, there is mounting pressure that nothing can relieve but work.

It is for this reason that artists so often fare poorly in talk therapy. Therapy ignores the need to work and focuses on the underlying cause of the need. "If we just figure out why you have to prove yourself, you won't have to prove yourself any longer," the thinking goes, but it does not go far enough. The urge to create is a primal human urge. It cannot be eliminated any more than the sex drive or the instinct for self-protection can.

An artist who is not working is a miserable creature, and the best way to cure that misery is to work. We do not have to work a lot. We do not have to work a long time, but we do need to work. The itch to make something is an itch that only making something will scratch. It doesn't need to be a good something—although it often is—it just needs to be something: a paragraph of prose, a rough sketch for a later painting, a stanza of poetry, the first verse of a song. In order to work freely, we must be willing to work badly, and once we are, we are often able to do good work indeed.

The smoke burns the eyes and chokes the throat. So, too, not working creates a discomfort that will not go away until we work. For an artist, not working sours an atmosphere just like smoke. It cannot be ignored for too long because the sheer physical discomfort becomes too much to take—the clenching of the stomach, the tightness in the chest, the tensing of jaw muscles—and not making art takes a physical toll on an artist. Conversely, when an artist is making art, there is a lightness to all other enterprises. Relationships sweeten. Temperaments unknot. It is uncanny, the simple joy of living that comes from putting in some time on our art.

"What's different?" people often will ask an artist who is happily working. "You look ten years younger. Did you have a facelift?" No, but we had a spirit-lift, and that is powerful indeed.

Vanity alone should make an artist work. The pride and self-enjoyment that comes from working translates across into all of our other endeavors. Other jobs come to us more easily when we are working. It is as though working on our art gives us energy rather than takes energy away. It is suddenly less of a chore to sort through that stack of papers, scrub out that tub, reorder the woodpile. When we work, we are often young at heart, and this youthful energy lingers with us after work is done.

JUST DO IT

Try this: Sometimes it is difficult to confront our work directly. We lack the nerve to look squarely at the course that lies ahead. This is our fear, and *all* artists have it. When we are fearful, it is best to sidle up to our next creative jump. Take pen in hand. Number from 1 to 5. List five actions that are indirectly related to your creative work. For example:

1. *Get the extra papers off my desk*
2. *Organize my work area*
3. *Wash and fold the laundry*
4. *Buy new artist supplies*
5. *Buy envelopes and stamps to make submissions*

Choose one action from your list and execute it.

Soldiering Through

THE DROUGHT TAKES ITS TOLL. Thirty miles to the north, Colorado is burning. Flames have formed a wall one hundred feet high. Homes have been devoured, as have great swaths of forest acreage. A woman has stepped forward to take the blame for the blaze. She angrily disregarded fire warnings to burn a letter from her estranged husband. The letter set the conflagration.

For the moment, Taos is out of harm's reach, although forty miles to the east, in Cimarron, a blaze has broken out and they are setting a counterfire to control it. The smoke from the counterfire is expected to be dense enough that those in Taos Ski Valley with respiratory ailments are asked to remain indoors for the next three days. This from a sign at the post office.

As with a forest fire, a creative drought can quickly become a destructive blaze destroying life, certainly quality of life, and property. There are those among us—myself numbered here—who write for a living. If the words won't come, the money can't follow, so the words must be kept flowing somehow.

In order to be able to write at all, and especially when pinched by a creative drought, we must be willing to write badly. This doesn't mean we necessarily will write badly, but that we are willing to write no matter what, to soldier through at the page even as our ego is shrieking, "This is terrible. You really cannot write!" And the same is true for the other arts as well.

It is always the ego, in the form of our inner perfectionist, that can be identified, like the letter burner, as the first cause of damage. The ego doesn't want us merely to be able to write, paint, sculpt, dance, or act. It wants us to do these things well, to do them brilliantly, or—and here is where drought sets in—not at all. Writer Tillie Olsen calls the perfectionist "the knife of the perfectionist attitude in art." She is accurate in this.

The perfectionist wants us to be able to work perfectly. It doesn't want to bother with rough drafts or sketches. It is out for the polished final product and it wants us to produce that first and all the time. It is the perfectionist's fingering the blade of the knife that keeps us from working much of the time. The perfectionist cajoles the ego into taking it seriously—and the ego, which wants desperately to control our art, is glad to have something in its power after all. The ego has the power to keep us from making art, but it does not really have the power to make art itself. Art is an act of the soul.

When we are in the grips of a creative drought, we do feel the knife blade at our throat. We do feel the demand, "Stay right where you are. Don't get fancy. You're not going anywhere." And the "not going anywhere" gets to be a habit.

The 12-step program Arts Anonymous—an excellent program—talks about the anorectic high that an artist can get from avoiding art. The fact that we are not making art becomes the obsessive something that fills our days. And make no mistake, "I'm not writing" takes up far more energy and space than "I am writing" ever will.

It takes humility to dismantle a creative block, and it takes the vigilant practice of humility to keep from building one. The ego wants to claim as much territory as we will allow it. "I am brilliant" is what the ego is after, not "I am of service," not "I am serviceable." And yet, it is in trying to be of service, in showing up at the page and listening rather than speaking, that we begin to make art that transcends the ego's brittle boundaries. At root, the ego is not an innovator. It wants its art to be validated, stamped with official approval. In this sense, it wants its art to be safe rather than daring.

When we are willing to make what wants to be made rather than make what we want, we become open to new directions. We begin to be able to let some of the seriousness out of our artist's life, and we begin to let some of the playfulness back in. It is an ironic fact that most great artists are inherently playful. As Carl Jung remarked, creativity is "the mind at play with the materials that it loves." This is a far cry from "production-line creativity."

The ego wants to be able to mass-produce excellence, but excellence is handcrafted. The ego wants to remove the elements of risk and daring and leave us with a sanitized version of art that is curiously castrated. A potent artist is a free artist, and a free artist is one who is able to work well or poorly with equal impunity. By being able to work poorly, we are free to innovate and to seek new ways of making our art. Just as modern dance embraces many previously awkward postures to create a new dance language, so, too, does ego-free art contain the freedom to embrace new forms.

SOLDIERING
THROUGH

Try this: Most artists unconsciously carry an inner perfectionist. This sentinel is often scornful and sarcastic, cutting us down to size whenever we seek to grow creatively larger. "Who do you think you are?" the perfectionist asks. "Do you *really* think you could pull that off?" Take pen in hand. Number from 1 to 10. Complete the following phrase as rapidly as possible:

1. *If my ego would allow it, I'd try*
   _____.

2. *If my ego would allow it, I'd try*
   _____.

3. *If my ego would allow it, I'd try*
   _____.

4. *If my ego would allow it, I'd try*
   _____.

5. *If my ego would allow it, I'd try*
   _____.

6. *If my ego would allow it, I'd try*
   _____.

7. *If my ego would allow it, I'd try*

   _____.

8. *If my ego would allow it, I'd try*

   _____.

9. *If my ego would allow it, I'd try*

   _____.

10. *If my ego would allow it, I'd try*

   _____.

As this brief exercise shows, there is often considerable creative territory that we yearn for, from which we allow our perfectionist to turn us aside. Select one risk from your list of ten.

Take a first step toward executing it.

When It Happens
to You

PIGEONS COO FROM THE EAVES of my old adobe house. We have done our best—the dogs and I—to convince them that they should nest elsewhere, but they are determined. They are here for the summer's duration, and no amount of pleading, cajoling, shooing, or barking can make them do anything as dramatic as leave. At most, they flap to a nearby telephone line, where they wait for us to calm down. Then, inexorably, they are back.

Just like the pigeons, a creative drought is a stubborn animal. It knows that it is not welcome, and it stays despite protests and attempts to move on. A creative drought is not budged by force. It does not yield to willpower. As artists, we have hardy wills, and we often use them to stay the course on long projects. But the will is of little use faced with the sheer wall of "I won't." And "I won't" is what the block says over and over again.

It feels like a boulder at the heart's door. A dark and heavy weight that blocks the sun and traps us in darkness. "Oh," we wail, newly chastened, "this is what they mean by creative block." It is as though all the stories we have ever heard of others' suffering, all the tales that left us sitting smugly—"That never happens to me!"—have now come home to roost.

"It will never happen to me" is the often unspoken but arrogant assumption that we make before block strikes us. We are like the children of alcoholics who say, "It will never happen to me," only to find themselves drinking as badly as ever their parent did.

Sometimes a block approaches on tiptoe. It gradually becomes harder and harder to write or to paint, until one day it is simply impossible. Other times a block strikes like a sudden blow, felling us instantly with its ferocity. One day you are sailing along, the next day—wham!—you are blocked. Your block may show itself as sudden fatigue or as a nervous energy that will not settle down to mere working. Your block will wear a mask at first so you do not know that it is your enemy. "It's just a bad day," you bravely mutter, but soon it is more than that. It is bad days strung together.

Very rapidly, your block becomes your dark and terrible secret. You carry it with you always. It is the dinner guest, the third party in your lover's bed. "What's wrong with you?" a beloved might wonder. We can barely summon the courage to say, "I'm blocked."

It is like the reverse of the alcoholic's experience. Instead of taking the drink whether we want to or not or even when we truly don't want to, we find we cannot work even when we desperately want to do it. We are just as powerless over the compulsion to not work as the alcoholic is over the compulsion to drink. And the solution, like the drunk's solution, must be spiritual. Drinking problems and blocks both yield only to a power greater than ourselves.

Am I saying that blocks dissolve in the light of prayer?

Yes. Blocks are not so much removed as evaded, and they are evaded by the strategy of letting God—or whatever you choose to call the force—work through us. We must resign as the conscious and self-congratulatory author. We must throw ourselves into work with a spiritual abandon. We must paint as though another hand holds the brush. We must surrender our ideas about what art is and where our art is going. We must become willing to be channels. We must allow the force that through the green fuse drives the flower to work through us.

"But, Julia, I don't believe in God," you may be saying. I was not certain that I believed in a God either until I got sober and had my first experience with being squarely blocked. Only in desperation did I become willing to try letting "it" work through me, and out of my desperation a certain ease was born. I simply wrote what was to be written and left the judgment of it to others. I worked at my craft—I worked daily—but I did it now not as the master but as the apprentice. I showed up at the page and listened rather than spoke. "Work through me" was my prayer. "Let me be a channel, a conduit, a pipe through which you flow, Great Creator."

I didn't know it then, but I later learned that I was praying as many artists before me had prayed. "Straightaway the ideas came in on me. Straight from God," Puccini recounted his writing of *Madame Butterfly.* And Beethoven, near suicide from the lack of reception for his work, vowed to live and write music for God alone to appreciate.

We have all appreciated these artists' prayers.

Ours is a secular time. We do not talk easily of God or of higher powers, the forces of inspiration that move through us as we work. And yet, the Great Creator is there, and so are benevolent helping forces, waiting only to be asked to step forward.

Try this: Remember, the way out of a creative block is through surrender, not conquest. We must first admit we *are* blocked, and then take appropriate actions. Admitting we are blocked is often difficult. It makes us feel too vulnerable for comfort. At root, a block is fear, and fear causes procrastination. Take pen in hand and list five areas in which you are procrastinating. For example:

1. *I haven't read my play since it got back from the typist*
2. *I haven't returned phone calls related to a job opening*
3. *I haven't written those letters of recommendation*
4. *I need to get my printer fixed*
5. *I haven't called my friend back about her book*

Take pen in hand again. Moving one at a time, write down your resentments, angers, and fears connected to each area in which you procrastinate. This tool is called Blasting Through Blocks, and it is quite powerful.

On a Dry Day

A RELENTLESS, prying wind blows in from the west. It carries clouds of smoke and ash, hazing over the far mountains. The drought is with us still, and the breeze provides only a temporary relief. The locals say that this is the wind that ages you, its feathery touch robs the cheek of moisture, it leaves the complexion furrowed and old. The Hispanic women wear hats and stay indoors, focused on housework. Their gardening gets done only at twilight, after the heat of the day. This is one stratagem they have adopted against the drought.

In times of creative drought, stratagems serve us. It is not a time for forcing growth. It simply doesn't work. Like the garden burned up from being watered at midday, when the water itself turns hot, we, too, can be burned up by forcing ourselves at an unnatural pace.

When we are unable to work, we can work at the work of getting ready to work. Writers can lay in supplies of paper and enticing pens, notepads that plead "Please write on me." Painters can prepare their canvases, clean their brushes, neaten their studio space. Potters can acquire a new lump of cool clay and clear the table space where they will knead and shape it. Gentle things can be done.

A creative doubt is at the root of all creative droughts. We have done as much as we can, we think, and we lack the heart to go further. We doubt our staying power and our genuine gift as an artist. Our faith in ourselves and often our faith in God has evaporated before the dry breeze of skepticism. We are worn out and we doubt that a "real artist" would be. And yet, all artists, "real artists" among them, suffer from droughts.

Often, though, a drought comes on the heels of a success. Second novels are notoriously hard to make, and second films too. We have met the jump once, and we do not think we have it in us to meet the jump again. And now the bar has been raised. There is the matter of expectations. This one "had better be good." We are wary of reviews and we review ourselves harshly and prematurely: "Not up to snuff."

Creative droughts come upon us just when we are "getting serious" about our art. Arguably, they come sweeping in on us because we are "getting serious" about our art. The fun has gone out of our process. We are focused on product, on "how am I doing?" The answer is, "not well," and the drought is the reason.

When we are "in the flow"—even the word speaks of water—ideas come to us naturally and we collect them like so many beautiful marbles, not even bothering in their abundance to hold them to the light. In a drought, ideas balk like stubborn horses. They refuse to come forward, or if they do, they come with ears flattened, tails lashing, teeth bared against our even thinking of making them serviceable mounts. A drought is a rebellion. We have pushed our inner creator too far and it is refusing to be pushed any further. "Back off," it is snarling, "leave me the hell alone."

In a drought, we have wounds to lick, and they are not always logical. A good review that leaves us stranded on the high rock of notoriety may be just as damaging as a foul review that has us slinking to the cave. Too much attention, good or bad, can tip us into drought. So can dragging home the invisible bone, doing a large and worthy piece of work only to have it go unreceived and unnoticed. "What's the use?" our inner creator asks then, and digs its heels in rather than risks making something more.

In a creative drought, we must approach ourselves indirectly. We must sidle up and coax, offer the wild horse an apple slice, if we are ever again to get a bridle on its head. We must prove ourselves safe and worthy if we are ever to regain the trust that ends a drought.

The road from Española to Taos coils through steep canyon. The Rio Grande, low this year from drought, flows alongside the road. Its tributary, the Embudo, is reduced to a nearly dry, rock-ribbed riverbed. A fine film of dust hangs in the air over the mountain passes. The wind from the west, insolent and harsh, parches the cottonwoods along the riverbank. Drivers drive erratically, half crazy from the sun and the glare. Travelers need caution.

When we are in a creative drought, we, too, need caution. We are dangerous to ourselves and others, time bombs looking for the opportunity to explode. Our nerves are hair-trigger. Small things annoy us. Small issues loom large as we blow things out of proportion. The big drama is that we are not working, but that drama is so painful that a thousand little dramas take its place. Suddenly, our perfect horse isn't perfect anymore. Our longtime friend is annoying. We seriously doubt everyone's loyalty. We are surrounded by fools, and we're foolish ourselves.

On the road through the canyon, an ancient truck is pulled to one shoulder, and down in the river its occupants can be seen cavorting in the shallow water. We can take a cue from them. The shallows can be enjoyed, not just endured. If we are too depressed for "serious" work, we can indulge in some serious play. We can rent a dumb movie. We can laugh to "Drew Carey" reruns. We can curl up with *Bridget Jones's Diary.*

Children's books are an excellent way to cajole a drought into ending. The Harry Potter series has probably launched a thousand novels by now. It is that high-spirited. And high spirits, high jinks, and laughter are the antidotes we are after. Remember, it was getting too serious that invited the drought in the first place. Getting unserious is part of what invites the healing rain.

We get "unserious" by getting little instead of big. I once ended an awful creative drought by writing a tiny song each day about animals. Every morning, after my Morning Pages, I would march myself to the piano. I would sit down and write: "Don't look now or you'll see an owl / The foulest fowl of the night / I am the one with the talons sharp / Who can see quite well in the dark. . . ." Progressing from owl through "a moose on the loose," I made myself and my inner creator laugh. By the time I was finished I had forty-five children's songs, a goodly album's worth, and my faith was restored in writing as a joyous art form.

In short, we can lean into our shallow selves. It's a good time for self-care. We book a masseuse, paint our toenails, go to the salon for a trim. Often, it is surprisingly hard to take it easy. Yet, taking it easy is what the situation calls for. With our temper frayed, it's difficult to be loving—to others and ourselves. It's easier to take out the sharp lash of judgment and whip ourselves into a frenzy over all we're not doing.

"I'm too tired," we may feel, and greet this feeling with "You're lazy." A smorgasbord of insults often follows. Lazy, grandiose, delusional, and, worst of all, boring—you'd think we *would* be bored with the litany by now. Navigating out of the canyon takes special care, and so does navigating our way free from drought. Others may pass us, horns blaring, but that does not mean our slow and steady pace should alter. Droughts make people crazy. They act in ways counter to their best selves. Coming out of the canyon, a pickup truck tailgates just to be certain you notice its impatience. Sometimes our friends tailgate us too. They are eager to have us back on our feet and functioning in ways comfortable to them. "I wish there were a pill you could take," they may volunteer. But no pill cures creative drought. Wise elders give us a wide berth, knowing we are in the briar patch, knowing we will need to work our way free in our own way and in our own time. Time itself is a touchy subject during a drought. Days loom long and empty, or are filled with the drudgery of ordinary tasks. Yet, time flees past as the days of not working mount up. Time feels like the enemy, and yet time is on our side. Time is working to heal us. Time will heal us, but in time.

ON A DRY DAY

Try this: Many of us set an impossibly high goal
of productivity for ourselves. We want to finish
the novel by next week, and if we can't do that,
we're a failure. We want the energy to work all
night, to burn the candle at both ends, no matter how exhausted and burned-out such behav-
iors leave us. When we set our creative jumps
too high, we often refuse to jump them. "Not
today," we say, and defer our creativity one more
day. It is better, and healthier, to set our creative
jumps within our creative reach. Take pen in
hand. Is there an arena in which you set your
goal impossibly high? Write about this. Having done a thorough inventory of your creative
self-sabotage, set a new creative quotient that you
will be able to meet with some ease. Take your
creative goal and plan it out. What do you want
to have done a year from now? Six months from
now? One month from now? One week from
now? Working "backward" in this way allows
you to set realistic creative goals.

Waiting for Water

STILL, the infernal wind blows. The sky is bleached by heat. Creek beds are empty. The sun glares down on the rock-ribbed beds. Bushes along the bank droop as if they have walked to water's edge and found it missing. The drought is inexorable.

And yet beneath the earth's parched surface, water courses in great, unchecked streams. The drought does not penetrate so deeply that all water is gone. It is the surface world that suffers. The peonies droop their snowy heads in the heat. The hollyhocks refuse to grow altogether. Hardy wildflowers, Indian paintbrush and the lot, make their way closer to civilization, and their beauty is a welcome relief. Drought leaches beauty from the land.

Make no mistake: When we are in a drought, what we are missing is joy. We miss the joy of creativity—our own—and we miss our joy in creation itself. "Oh, look," we think dully, "a beautiful rose. So what?" It is the "so what?" aspect that makes a drought so debilitating. It makes any attempts to cheer us up fall flat. We are depressives when we are blocked. The good, the beautiful, the joyous cannot touch our grief-hardened hearts. Yes, I did say "grief-hardened," because grief is another variable present in all blocks. We are caught by the throat with sorrow over what we are missing in the world and in ourselves. We feel we have let ourselves down—and everyone else along with us. We simply are impostors, fakes in artists' clothing.

We cannot lift a finger to make art, and we may have trouble lifting a finger to do anything—the laundry or our hair.

What we need to use our fingers for when we are in drought is to soothe our fevered brow. "There, there," we must whisper to ourselves. "It will be all right. It will be all right." And it will be all right, but not if we ask too much too soon, not if we badger and prod and poke at ourselves. We are invalids—notice that the word says in-valid—and that is how we feel. Any activity that can be broached must be broached gently. "Try just a little," we must offer ourselves, as though we were spooning in hot chicken soup.

When we are in a creative drought, we feel bereft of comfort, robbed of beauty. We are the unenchanted ones. Even when beauty passes by, it leaves us unmoved. Like the rains that will not come, when we are in a drought, our hearts will not leap up. We are seized by a rebellion against all that would nurture and comfort us. We rotisserie in our misery: blocked. We are blocked.

What does blocked feel like—other than bad? Blocked feels like nothing else. A blocked artist is a numb artist, a grief-locked animal caught in its own torpor and resistance, the way soldiers return from bloody war, traumatized by what they have seen. We would move, we would be interested, but we cannot—just now— and our fears whisper that we will never be quickened by beauty and passion again.

When we are in a drought, our great fear is that the rain will never come. We scan the horizon for any signs of water, and we come back to ourselves still hopeless, helpless, and dry. We cannot force our work. We cannot make it rain. But we can remember that there is water coursing under the earth's parched crust and there is creativity in us, deep inside, a great underground river of creativity that will once again bubble to the surface, that will, eventually, let us work.

It is a great comfort to know that our creativity is not gone— merely gone underground. It is a comfort to know that it waits for us and that we can wait for it as well. During times of drought, we can ease our suffering by remembering gentleness. Gentleness is the key to survival. We must move slowly with ourselves. We must treat ourselves as war veterans, survivors, and we must tend to ourselves with care.

Just as a sick friend may be coaxed to eat, we may be ever so gently coaxed into remembering our creative loves. If we drew horses with passion and acuity, then we can gently leaf through books on the horse. We do not need to draw, yet. We need to draw nurturance instead. The act of looking at what we love, remembering what we love, connects us delicately to the underground streams we are seeking to reach.

If we are a poet who has no poems, we can turn to reading beloved poets. We can read children's books of verse. We can wallow a little in doggerel, bad poetry of the sort we are afraid we just might write—if we were writing at all, that is. If Neruda or Lowell or Whitman or Wright leaves you still unstirred, if a venture into Roethke doesn't wake your poet to smiling, then it is time for something easier. Read novels, even bad and lurid novels. Write postcards or letters even if all they do is complain about the fact that you are not writing. It is better to lodge that complaint in writing. It is fair, too, to write a letter to God bewailing your fate and God's cruelty and caprice, dragging you away from your beloved, casting you into ashy darkness, causing you to suffer so.

And we do suffer when we are in drought. We haul out long lists of words that we use to whip our hapless shoulders. We are "lazy," we tell ourselves, "untalented," an "impostor," "phony," "fake," "shallow," a "has-been." We do not say what might be the God's truth: "I am resting. I am gathering steam. I am in a low cycle, a time of dormancy, a period in which I will come to know exactly how much and how deeply I love the art I am not able at the moment to practice."

If absence imbues the retreating beloved with radiance, then our hearts burn with the love we hold for the art we feel is denied us. Caught in the grip of a creative drought, we remember when words or images flowed freely. We remember when we acted with grace, commitment, and abandon. We remember and we doubt that we will ever again be so blessed. We doubt that the drought will ever end, that the moist wind of inspiration will ever blow, that we will have a moment of grace when an idea will bubble up unbidden and we will act on it with ease and alacrity.

Droughts are dramatic and apocalyptic, and when we are in them, so are we. "It's all over," we tell ourselves—and anyone else who will listen. "I can't write, and it's killing me." "I'm not painting." "I am at the end of my road as a sculptor." "I'm all washed up as an actor." Although we may know enough to suspect that drama, per se, is spurious, each new bout of drama is astoundingly convincing.

We are certain—or we at least suspect—that the direst and most bleak prospects are the true ones, the ones that wait to mug us in that dark alley known to us as our future.

Because of our pain, we greet optimism with suspicion and derision. "You'll be writing again before the end of the month," someone tells us. We think, "The end of *what* month?" "You'll paint again, maybe by Sunday," a well-wisher volunteers, and we know he does not understand that we have been struck color-blind, unable to love and respond to the amaryllis red we have squeezed from our paint tube. Cerulean blue is just a tint to us in our flattened condition. Ochre cannot seduce us, nor wonderful pine green. All of that is dead to us, we insist. And we insist the way you push on a sore tooth for the thrill of it, the way you press a purpling bruise to wince again with pain.

"I am injured," we insist—and we are right about that. We are injured—not maimed, as we fear. Not crippled for life, as we dread. But temporarily stiff and sore and aching all over as if we had a very bad case of the flu, the kind that makes you feel like death warmed over—and not warmed up enough at that.

What we need is a Florence Nightingale, a ministering angel who sees our pain and doesn't discount it. We need to be babied a little and in just the right way. We need our ministering angel to whisper that the dark night we are passing through will end and that it will prove to be fruitful no matter how it now appears.

"Of course you are frightened, of course you are worried," we need to be told. "That's so natural in a drought. Who would you be if you didn't worry? What kind of artist if you didn't miss your art?"

Our creativity never leaves us. Sometimes, however, its surface appearance fades away. We become parched with longing for our work, but our sources of strength are now not our easy tricks. We are being humbled and opened for greater work to come through us, and that humility feels to us like humiliation, that opening-up feels like a gaping wound. We are deathly afraid that art has left us alone forever, that we will never see the beloved's face or feel its simple touch.

"I was such a fool," we think. "I took so much for granted." And we did. But faced with our drought, we don't any longer, and this is the beginning of humility and honesty. It is the beginning of emptying ourselves so art can again pour through us.

WAITING FOR
WATER

Try this: When we are creatively stymied, most of us fall into self-flagellation rather than work on self-love. Our spirit is already discouraged by our lack of productivity, and we discourage it further by accusing ourselves of lack of character. We are "lazy," "unfocused," "mere dilettantes." Such self-attack does little to move us forward. At best, we work grudgingly and under half steam. Take pen in hand. Number from 1 to 10. Complete the following phrase as rapidly as possible:

1. *Something I really love doing is*
   _____.

2. *Something I really love doing is*
   _____.

3. *Something I really love doing is*
   _____.

4. *Something I really love doing is*
   _____.

5. *Something I really love doing is*
   _____.

6. *Something I really love doing is*

      _____.

7. *Something I really love doing is*

      _____.

8. *Something I really love doing is*

      _____.

9. *Something I really love doing is*

      _____.

10. *Something I really love doing is*

      _____.

From your list of beloved activities, select the one that sounds the most fun now. Do that one. *Then* turn back to work.

Keep Moving

IT IS YET ANOTHER DAY of drought in northern New Mexico. The bright sun beats down from a pale blue sky. A few high and fluffy white clouds graze like sheep, but they are not the kind of clouds that clot together and mean rain. No, rain will elude us for another day, and the best plan is simply to accept it.

Sometimes in our creative careers we are seized by a sickening rebellion. We think, "I simply cannot keep on with keeping on," and so we skid to a halt. The halt becomes like the drought, daily taking a deeper hold on our psyches until we're defined by the absence of work, just as a drought is defined by the absence of water.

A day of not working, like a day of no rain, is uncomfortable and, after a time, unbearable. The only way out of drought is rain, which will come when God or providence declares it should. The only way out of a creative drought is through our own hand, and that we have some slight measure of power over.

We can take to the page and write, "I am not working. I am unwilling to work. I hate working and I have no ideas left." That is like a prayer for rain. It moves the heavens somehow. We can post a sign in our workplace that says: "I am willing to work badly," and then we can work despite how sluggish and ill-formed we judge the resulting work to be.

In times of creative drought, the only solution is to keep putting one foot in front of the other, to keep on slogging creatively, to keep moving toward a distant horizon. We are like people crossing a vast desert. Water lies ahead and not behind. It lies in our future and not in our present. We must move toward it when every footfall seems a mockery. And why must we keep on moving?

We must keep moving because all droughts end. The parched earth is slaked by rain, and the parched creative spirit is slaked, too, when the long months of forced work give way suddenly to the verdant flowering of inspiration.

Sometimes we forget that art is a spiritual path and that all spiritual journeys are characterized by time in the desert. We want our art to flow as easily as a mountain stream, and we remember with bitterness the days when it did flow and we were ungrateful— unconscious, really, why we should be grateful. The days will come again when our art will flow freely and when we will be seized and carried away by inspiration. We help those days to come more easily if we keep the faith and keep working, however slowly and tentatively, through our periods of drought.

As artists, we are married to our work. We have a commitment to it for better or for worse, in sickness and in health, until death do us part. Sometimes the marriage will be filled with heady romance. We will know we have chosen the right, most intoxicating partner. Other days, the romance will wear thin or disappear altogether. We will find ourselves stubbornly and unwillingly yoked to a partner who seems cold or barren or foreign to us. Our bond will feel like servitude, like a robbery of life that could surely flow in other directions. But could it?

At root, as artists, we have an obligation to make art. Art is what fulfills our deepest natures. Art is what gives our life a sense of godliness and right direction. Art is what we make so that at the end of each day we can say, "At least I made X today," and feel some satisfaction. There are probably people who are not called to make art. They make their satisfaction from relationships or some other dutiful labor that speaks to them of mission—family, job, community. For us, as artists, family, job, and community are all served best by our continuing devotion to the muse that calls us to art. After that obligation is fulfilled, all others cheerfully follow. Until that obligation is met, everything else is forced, empty, grudging.

As artists, we wish we could always work well, but we must settle for working always. The "always" we can control. The "well" we cannot control. For this reason, we do well to simply serve, to focus more on the process of doing our work than on the "product" of work produced. Judgment will come soon enough.

There is a mercy inherent in working. It is as though the heavens give us just a little moistening rain whenever we bend to the wheel of our art. A sense of accomplishment and rightness settles over our spirit, a sense of dignity and right action. We may not have worked "well," but we have worked. We have cooperated with the Great Creator by being creative ourselves.

KEEP MOVING

Try this: Often when we skid to a halt in our work, we skid to a halt in our spiritual life as well. We do not think to ask God's help to dissolve our creative resistance, and yet such prayer is often the right answer. Take pen in hand and pray on the page. Write a letter to whatever you conceive of as the Great Creator. Complain, gripe, moan, sigh, weep, scream in sheer frustration. And ask for help. Next, pick up the phone and call an open-minded and positive friend. Explain that you need spiritual support for your creative endeavor. Ask her to pray for your restored productivity. Finally, go back to work. Your prayers have been answered, and you have achieved enough mobility to give work a try.

Hope

YESTERDAY WE HAD a few drops of rain, a slight teaser just misting the sky. "Rain will come," it promised. "The drought will end." All about this tiny town, Taos, the little splash of rain was the big event. "Did you get any rain?" was the question people asked one another as they met. By "rain" they meant even a soupçon, the barest, merest drizzle. Such rain, scanty as it was, brought hope.

Hope is elusive for many of us. We lead lives mired in dailiness. We wish for change. We wish for expansion, but we have scant hope that change and expansion can come to us—and yet they can, often as just the smallest sprinkling at first.

In archaic times, "hope" meant "trust or reliance." In its current usage it means "desire accompanied by expectation or belief in fulfillment." Viewed this way, hope is linked to faith. If we believe in no God, or a withholding God, we will have little faith that our dreams will come true and therefore little hope. If we believe in a benevolent God, one who is friendly to our dreams and goals, then it is easier to have faith and therefore hope. In other words, hope or the lack of hope is directly linked to our faith or lack of faith.

We have built our lives a step at a time, making choices that have left us fulfilled or unfulfilled. Most of us have arenas in which we wish to expand further, and in those arenas we have need of faith and hope. "I would love to write a novel" is one such hope.

We may or may not have the faith to begin. "I would love to paint more often," another dream might run. Again, whether we start or not will depend on our faith in being able to continue. It is often not so much that we doubt our ability to begin as it is that we doubt our ability to continue. We lack faith in ourselves and therefore we lack the hope that our dreams can come true.

When we imagine a God of partnership, it is easier to have hope. With a partnering God, projects are completed in tandem, with a helping hand always at the ready. "I believe; help my disbelief," we pray, and in so praying we are led a step at a time.

One of the reasons it is wise to find creative colleagues is that often our friends can see the hand of guidance where we cannot. As we are focused on what is missing, a true friend may be focused on what is found. "I need a really good director," we might be thinking, despairing of encountering such an animal. Our friend, meanwhile, can remind us, "A month ago you needed a really good agent, and you found her. Why should finding a director be any different?"

It is easy to focus on what we haven't got and on what we still need. It is more difficult, a learned skill, to focus on what has come into place, how far we have already traveled on the road we are seeking to follow. For many of us, the words "I hope" have a certain desperation about them, as if we are saying, "I hope against hope," but our prayers are answered. Our dreams are fulfilled. Our needs are met. There is a benevolent Something that leans toward us, mentoring and sheltering our dreams, but we must be willing to see this help, willing to acknowledge it, willing to count our blessings and not discount them as they come to us.

Twelve-step programs talk about the importance of an "atti-

tude of gratitude." This is no mere bromide. When we practice
counting our blessings, our blessings multiply. The very act of saying "thank you" opens the heart another notch in receptivity.
Receptivity is pivotal in allowing our dreams to be fulfilled. We
cannot force our way in this world but we can allow the world
to help us. It is in the allowing, this vulnerable openness, that so
many of us fall short. Rather than daring to hope for an answered
prayer, we close our minds and our hearts to the help that comes
to us in a thousand forms.

We often decide that our help must take a certain shape and
come to us from a certain person or institution. We know where
we want to go and we think we know how we should go there.
This is where our faith wears thin. We do not really believe we will
be helped and so we are blind to the help that takes an unexpected
form. Our goal may be a produced Broadway show and our need
may actually be a producer before a director, but we can be too
willfully blind to see that course adjustment as it is made by "the
Fates."

If we believe that there is a kindly Someone or Something that
is interested in helping us manifest our dreams, then we need to be
willing to relinquish some control as to just how. This relinquish-
ing of control is a sticking point for many of us. We pray, "Please
help me, and let me tell you how" rather than "Please help me.
Thy will be done." It is difficult to rationally bolster our stubborn
independence. We ask that the Lord of all, the maker of galaxies
and flowers, take an interest in our life, and then we try to dictate the
form that help should take. Why not trust that the Great Creator,
limitless in creative power, might have the right solution for us and
our difficulties?

There is one divine mind working through all and in all. When we consciously acknowledge that fact and ask that our own dreams and projects be manifested as part of the divine unfolding, then we are on the right track. We are open again to mystery as well as mastery. We are taking our proper place as a creation amid creation, a divine idea that continues divine thought by plans and projects of our own. Our will and God's will are not inimical. Our dreams and God's dream for us are not so different. In fact, our heart's dream and the dream of God may be the same. We can hope so, and in our hope we can trust that our dreams will be fulfilled.

Try this: It is often difficult to admit our hopes.
They are tied so closely to our dreams. And yet,
the first step in answered prayer is to make a
prayer, and we can pray best when we are willing to be authentic. Take pen in hand. Number
from 1 to 10. Complete the following phrase as
rapidly as possible:

   1. *I hope that* _____.
   2. *I hope that* _____.
   3. *I hope that* _____.
   4. *I hope that* _____.
   5. *I hope that* _____.
   6. *I hope that* _____.
   7. *I hope that* _____.
   8. *I hope that* _____.
   9. *I hope that* _____.
  10. *I hope that* _____.

Our hopes range from the very small to the
very large. It is important that we remember
that the Great Creator is large enough to fulfill
all our hopes, whatever their size. When we rely
on the benevolent abundance of the Great Creator rather than on our own limited resources,
our hopes become answered prayers.

Seasonality

IT IS A SULTRY MIDSUMMER'S DAY. Small apples bob in the trees. The willow waves in the breezes. Overhead, magpies and ravens dart and float. The valley is peaceful. The slight rains have laid the dust devils to rest. The air carries moisture again, and the heat is touched by cool. This is the high desert, after all, and when we have cooling rains, the altitude shows in our temperatures. Last night the Ski Valley was chilly, and late-night concertgoers clutched their sweaters against the brisk night air. A high mountain stream rippled alongside the concert hall, contributing its own music to the night. The drought may be over.

Those who are seasoned in creative endeavors know that creative droughts, too, are passing things. Work long enough and gently enough, continue working when it is hard and feels impossible, and the reward will come sooner or later—the energy will rise again, ideas will flow, and work will one more time become a pleasure.

There is a seasonality, a cyclicity, to creative work. There are ripening times of midsummer, when our ideas bob in our heads like a good crop of apples. There is fall, the time of harvest, when we take those ideas down and collect them. There is a wintertime, when our ideas feel ice-locked and dormant and we must wait them out, writing Morning Pages each day, and then there is spring, the stirrings of new ideas and new directions.

Because the seasons of creativity are so varied, they can be frightening. In spring we can doubt our budding ideas will come to anything. In summer we can worry about our ability to keep up. In fall we may fear that we will not harvest our ideas successfully, that we will bruise them as we try to bring them home. In winter we may fear that we will never work again, and use the long, quiet times to beat ourselves up over the creativity that seems gone, not merely dormant.

Most veteran artists know that it is good to work at work even when the work is not working. Seasoned novelist John Nichols writes daily just to stay in shape. I write daily for the same reason. My sister, Libby, a painter, gets in at least one daily sketch and never allows time to build up when she is not in her studio. Sick, she sketches in bed. Such gentle forward-moving activity is a learned husbandry. It is easier to work again if you have never really stopped.

Sophie, a newer writer, tends to lapse into terrifying silences between books. "I am not writing, not writing anything!" she will wail. I have tried urging her to write Morning Pages, reminding her that a little trickle of writing keeps the flow from closing down completely, but this is a lesson she doesn't want to learn and so she endures a repeated drama: "I will never write again. I am really not a writer after all." This, despite five books to the contrary.

Artists have active imaginations, and we must learn to turn them toward the positive. Left to their own devices, our imaginations predict horrifying creative downfalls, dry spells, droughts, permanent blocks. This is why creative visualization is such a valid tool for artists—it points our imagination down more halcyon paths. "Imagine an ideal day" or "Picture yourself working at the height of your powers." It can feel foreign and threatening to try to foresee not creative catastrophe but the successful culmination of our dreams. A daydream of collecting a Tony award or an Oscar can seem like grandiosity. Meanwhile, we seldom curtail our day-dreaming of bad reviews. We call that "realism," but is it?

Someone needs to succeed in the arts. Why not you? Some-one's novel will be published. Why not yours? Someone's screen-play will be produced. Why not yours? Indeed, it could be argued that we must conceive success to be possible in order to have it.

I would suggest that the action of positive imagination is the first action that we should take. Think of it as a kind of magnetic grid, a form that invites success to come and fill it. In spiritual terms this can be phrased: Ask, believe, receive. When we imagine ourselves to be successful in our art, we are asking for success. Not all prayers need to be uttered aloud. When we allow our imagina-tions to inhabit the positive, we are believing and calling success to our sides. When we open our minds to our success, we become able to receive it. Without such open-mindedness, we turn our gifts away.

Let us allow our gifts to ripen instead. Let us plan to harvest our successes like the autumn apples, so ripe they fall to the touch. Let us believe in abundance and appreciate it even as it comes to our side. The prayer of "thank you" for blessings received and blessings anticipated is a very powerful prayer. "Oh, *grazie,* oh, thank you," we can say to the Great Creator, and let that anthem lift our hearts and minds to the many miracles possible.

SEASONALITY

Try this: When we refuse to honor the seasonality of our creative lives, we are often frustrated. We push too hard and too fast, and we torment ourselves over our lack of continuous productivity. Take pen in hand. Number from 1 to 5. List five projects you are involved in, and the season you are at in each. For example:

1. *Learning to play the piano (spring: I'm just starting out)*
2. *Weight loss (summer: I've made good progress, my diet is going well)*
3. *Writing a new musical (spring: I'm just gathering ideas)*
4. *Finishing a musical (fall: I'm in the final draft/rewrite phase)*
5. *Starting another novel (winter: This area of my creativity feels dormant right now)*

Scanning your list, allow yourself to realize the type and amount of creative effort appropriate to the season of your projects.

Allowing Guidance

As I write, the soft and downy fluff from cottonwood trees floats past my writing room window, dancing above the peak of the rusted tin roof that crowns my old adobe home. Wafting in on a breeze so slight it seems nonexistent, the tiny puffs are like the thoughts we have about how our life could be better. The thoughts, like the cottonwood fluff, float in from nowhere and dance on the edge of our consciousness. "I would love to . . ." they might begin, or, "Wouldn't it be fun to try . . ."

Most of us are adroit at ignoring such gentle thoughts. We swat them out of our consciousness, saying, "Not now. I'm too busy" or "Not now. I don't see how it can be done."

A great deal of the time we dismiss our longings on the grounds that they aren't reasonable—and often they aren't. Where did we get the idea that life was intended to be reasonable? And where would we be if Columbus, for example, had listened to reason?

We have very little evidence that sensible and frugal are actually qualities cherished by the Great Creator. A quick glance at creation is enough to show us that flowers number in the thousands, that butterflies do the same, and that something had a great deal of glee creating things that weren't, strictly speaking, necessary. Perhaps we need to believe a little more in this generous and prodigal

God. Perhaps we need to think about whether this Great Creator might not back some of our crazy schemes before we dismiss them out of hand as impossible or unreasonable.

Magellan was obsessed with finding a strait through the Americas that might lead to the isles of spice. He sought help from the king of Portugal, who turned a deaf ear. Finally, owing more allegiance to his dream than to his nation, he agreed to sail for Spain. Setting out to sea with five boats and a mission that was deemed foolhardy and impossible, the great navigator did circumnavigate the globe, proving once and for all that the world was round and that you could reach the east by sailing to the west.

Not all of us are Magellan, obsessed with some great enterprise, but most of us have a dream that we could set sail if only we dared. We would like to write a novel. We dream of sculpting. We want to build a darkroom in our garage. We want to tackle a certain concerto that eludes our hungry fingers. Rather than act on these dreams, we often shoo them from our consciousness, saying, "I need to be sensible. I would never be able to manage that."

But perhaps we can manage much more than we think. Perhaps there really is an unseen force that swings into action when we dare to pursue a dream. The phrase "a wing and a prayer" describes the uncanny sense pilots have that God is their copilot. For those of us who are earthbound, the phrasing might run "God is my cocreator."

When we commit to a dream, some great gate swings open and people and events surge forward to us in the form of supplies. As we hold steady to our dream, the materials needed to build that dream come to hand for us, and this is true whether our dream is writing musical comedy or building a new church.

Eight years ago I began writing music. I had no training musically. All I had were the vast swaths of melody and lyrics that swept through my head. I wanted to write a musical, but the odds of succeeding seemed as remote as Africa, and just as dark and forbidding. Nonetheless, I went to work, writing my music as an alphabetical code that could later be translated into notes. Whenever the work seemed the most impossible, some new bolt of music would announce itself—glorious and imperious, demanding "Write me." Feeling I was truly crazy, I obeyed, filling notebook after notebook with lyrics and "code."

Fortunately, I am friends with a wonderful psychic named Sonia Choquette, the author of five books on the power of belief in the unseen.

"You're not crazy," Sonia told me. "You're musical. And if you keep at it, I see a woman coming into your life to help and teach you—if you allow it. Why don't you try to allow it?"

And so I kept working at the music and the music kept working at me, and eventually I was able to stage a small workshop production of musical number one, *Avalon*. The production was held on a tiny auditorium stage in Taos, New Mexico—if not the middle of nowhere, certainly the middle of nowhere very likely. To the opening-night performance came a visiting New Yorker, a woman named Emma Lively, the very woman Sonia had foreseen my meeting and working with. Deftly as a hand slips into a glove, Emma slipped into my life. My alphabetic code did not baffle her. She quickly transcribed it and unfurled it into music. For four years now, we have worked together, and some three hundred songs, including two full-scale musicals and two children's albums, are the result. And even as I write this essay, I hear music pouring from

Emma's piano, music that I wrote and despaired of ever hearing realized.

So it is from my own experience that I know that dreams can come into being that are far larger and grander than we dare to hope. Help can come to hand that is far more accurate and deft than we dared to ask for. Guidance can unfold a step at a time so that the cottonwood fluff of our fancies becomes the reality we hold in our lives. "Thy will be done" is the prayer that allows us to allow this greater unfolding. Our eventual size is perhaps none of our business. We may all be far larger and more beautiful than we ever dare imagine. Like the cottonwood fluff, we can be lifted on high by invisible breezes that float us to our dreams.

ALLOWING
GUIDANCE

Try this: We are all directly connected to an inner and higher source of wisdom. We access this wisdom through Morning Pages and through the use of what might be called "guided writing." Consider this task an exercise in open-mindedness. Take pen in hand. Pose a question in an area where you need guidance. Listen quietly and write down the advice that you hear. This form of inner dialogue is very useful, and most people find they can easily access a wisdom that appears greater than their own.

Keeping On

THE AIR IN TAOS VALLEY is silvery with smoke. To the south, in the Sangre de Cristos, a fresh fire rages near Truchas. Firefighting is made far harder by the noisome winds pushing the flames along with ember-laden gusts. The miracle shrine, Santuario de Chimayo, lies not far from the blaze. So far, prayers for a respite seem to be going unanswered. My friend Elberta, with her horse farm in nearby Española, stands ready to receive evacuated horses. How bad the blaze will be is still unknown, but the high mountain pastures, baked by the sun and raked by the wind, are quick tinder.

We haven't had a drought like this in a hundred years, or in thirteen, depending on who you believe. A long time either way. The elders cluck and advise precautions. No smoking out-of-doors, no watering of lawns and gardens, no lengthy showers, no wasting the precious little water we have left. To the elders, such a gentle discipline comes naturally. They know that our actions matter, and that our cooperation with the Fates wins us a more merciful passage through difficult times.

During periods of creative drought, the same gentle husbanding of resources yields results. The careful daily turning to the page, recording there our frustrations and angers, yields us a way to carry on without setting a match to our dissatisfaction.

David, a young writer in between short stories, writes his Morning Pages daily, saying, "I wish I had another story idea." His wish is a written prayer, and its answer comes to him in the impulse to work on a new idea, to write down a scrap of dialogue he overhears, to send a long, meandering letter to a friend. All writing primes the pump.

Casey, a veteran writer, writes daily despite feelings of hopelessness and despair. "I am not sure I have another book in me," Casey tells his intimates. Writing for the sake of writing, he improves his odds. "I am a writer, and writers write," Casey sums up his credo. At sixty, Casey has endured green years and lean years, years of publishing and years of quiet. "I'm stubborn," Casey says, making light of the long years of daily writing practice.

If we examine any lengthy artistic career, we will discover the stubborn thread of perseverance. Oscar Hammerstein endured a ten-year drought in between his early success with Jerome Kern and his later success with Richard Rodgers. Throughout the decade of public failure, he hewed to a private practice of writing, working at his craft even when his career appeared to be in ashes.

Where and how do we find the resources to keep on keeping on? We look for them within our hearts. Just as the earth contains great underground rivers, we, too, contain unsuspected inner resources. In easy times, swept along by shared enthusiasms and outward success, we often work lightly, without knowing the depth of our own nature. It takes hard times to bring out our inner hardiness.

At eighty-two, director John Newland directed my play *Four Roses,* a six-woman piece set in an alcoholic treatment center. When we wrapped the production, Newland scheduled an immediate lunch to discuss what we might do next. He broached plans for an acting class, eager, as always, to keep working. Newland was thirty years my senior, and greeted my fears of aging with laughter and a challenge. "Why, I did my best work after fifty," he told me. "You're just a kid."

At eighty-two, Max Showalter traveled from Connecticut to Taos, where I was teaching a creativity camp. "You have to be positive," he explained. "You just have to be." Seated at the piano, performing for an audience of campers, he tinkled the keys and regaled the crowd with his tales of just keeping on.

It takes courage to be persistent, courage to try one more time—and then once again. What Casey calls his "stubbornness" is actually his courage. Courage is from the French word *coeur,* "heart." When John Newland told me to "take heart," it was a direction, not a bromide. We take heart when we commit to ourselves. To make art one more day.

The fire near Truchas fills the air with great plumes of smoke. Some pale as powder, some dark as ash. At Elberta's horse farm, business runs as usual. Some horses rotated to pasture, other horses put through their paces, still other horses on a day's sabbatical. The result of all the careful care is a string of glossy show horses ready to take championships. All of the training boils down to a gentle discipline, a daily doing and redoing. For us as artists, the regime must be the same.

Outside my writing room window stands a graceful, stately willow. The willow has flourished by sending deep roots into the earth under the acequia, a small water ditch. In this year's drought, the acequia stands empty, but moisture is still locked deep in the earth below its dry bed, and the willow, fresh and green, stands testament to this.

In making a life in the arts, we need roots like the willow, far-reaching enough to compensate us for a season's dry time. Our friendships form such a system, grounded in goodwill that reaches beyond each season's success or failure. When we seek those friendly to our art, we seek those compassionate to its process. When they ask, "How is it going?" the answer can be more than a litany of recent wins.

I have a friend, Bernice, who is friendly toward my music. When we talk, she inquires about my music the way one might inquire of a child's health. "And how is your music, Julia?" Bernice will say. "I feel like it comes from some high, fine place. Are you writing any music of the Southwest?" The very question sets me humming.

KEEPING ON

Try this: Many of us would love to keep on if we could just figure out how. We forget that Morning Pages, Artist Dates, and Walks are all tools that move us forward. Instead of seeking small and gentle next steps, we look for dramatic breakthroughs. Take pen in hand and list five *tiny* ways by which you could move forward.

For example:

1. *Morning Pages*
2. *Artist Dates*
3. *Walks*
4. *Straightening my work area*
5. *Subscribing to a magazine in my area of interest*

The point of this list is gentle encouragement, but embedded in that word is the root word *courage*. Take heart and execute one tiny step forward.

Remembering Who
We Are

THE WICKED WIND IS LESS TODAY. The sky is still silvered over with dust, but the world is not as beset. The large fire burning near Truchas appears to be safely contained and, unless there is a sudden switch in the ever-treacherous wind, it may burn itself safely out, sparing the old village. Of course, rain, real rain, would help.

This morning when I woke up, the mountain was erased. Smoke from the Truchas fire had plumed skyward and then settled down like a still, dense fog. We could have been in the Midwest. All that was visible was flatland. The looming mountains were lost to view. It was an eerie feeling, driving into town. The mountains were simply gone. I caught myself thinking how often we undergo such psychological tricks where the mountains of all we have done, been, and accomplished are invisible to our eyes, when we make ourselves out to be much flatter than we are.

The soul is beautiful and colorful. It expresses itself in our lives as tenderness and beauty. All of us have friendships that we cherish and nurture carefully. All of us have areas in our lives where we have brought harmony and beauty—the well-raised daughter or son, the beloved pet, the carefully kept and clean home. No life is empty of some shining spot where grace and concern have brought godliness.

How much better might our lives feel if we remembered to

acknowledge these invisible mountains of self-worth? What if we focused a little less on what we "should" do and counted a little more on what we have done? In short, what if we practiced a gentle gratitude toward our spirit for having tried so hard and in so many ways to be honorable? Self-appreciation is a discipline, and it is grounded in a sense of self-worth. We must believe that we are worthy of our own approval, and then we must give it to ourselves consciously and concretely.

We can start with something small. For example, "I am pretty good at staying in touch with my friends." Yes, we can always be "better," but that is not the point here. The point is acknowledging what may already be good enough. Try again: "I keep a pretty house."

For most of us, these positive affirmations, however modest, will be met with an objection. Good with your friends? "You haven't called Laura lately." A pretty house? "All the geraniums need to be pruned back." Where does this cruelty come from? Why is it so hard to praise ourselves, to love ourselves just as we are?

A great deal of the difficulty in making art springs from this conviction that what we are at any given moment is not enough. We want to be better, wiser, more ready to write before we write. We want to be more in the mood, more inspired, more alive before we try to paint. And yet, over long years of work, it is clear that some of the best writing comes through when we are not feeling struck with light. Some of the finest painting gets done on the days when we just show up at the easel because that is our job. In other words, when we practice self-acceptance of where we are and who we are instead of striving, always, to be better.

We are enough, exactly as we are.

It is very easy to forget our divine origins. It is very easy to see ourselves as the products of our birth families, shaped and colored only by those transactions. We are much larger than that. We are each a soul, unique and distinctive, bringing to bear on life a rich legacy of spiritual gifts if we but open ourselves to the possibility that we are not merely the products of our conditioning. We are spiritual beings with spiritual business to transact here on this earth. We have a destiny to fulfill.

When we chronically criticize ourselves, it makes it difficult for us to take action. We freeze, afraid that we are liable to do something badly. We do not risk that in fact we may do it well and that we may be the one person intended to do the good deed we are avoiding. Take, for example, the conversation you might have urging a gifted student to have the self-worth to go on to college. Perhaps you alone can reach this young person's heart. I am thinking now of a talented actor who met retired film director John Newland in the unlikely backwater of Taos. Assessing the youngster's talent, Newland immediately steered him toward an acting conservatory on the coast. "You don't want to be stuck here as a big fish in a small pond. You can be a big fish in a big pond," Newland told him.

We intersect one another's lives for a purpose, and we bear gifts for one another. When we are hypercritical of ourselves, we are afraid to offer the gifts that we bear, gifts of acknowledgment and appreciation, gifts of acceptance and respect. Focused on criticizing the self, it is hard to offer help or guidance to others. It creates a vicious cycle. We feel small, we act small, and then we conclude that we are small because we have shirked the largeness required of us.

Self-acceptance makes it easier for us to be large.

How do we work, then, to accept ourselves? It begins with a

determination to remember the beauty of our own personality. There are many days when our mountains are erased by the haze of low self-worth. Reminding ourselves that our glorious mountains are real, that we have acted well and will act well again, is a step in the right direction. It also helps to sneak up on self-worth. Begin with comments to the self that are less threatening. Perhaps you can edge from "I am kind" to "I am generous." Admitting that we are kind and generous, we can, perhaps, then take a kind and generous action that reinforces the notion that we are kind and generous. We can return the phone call we have been dodging out of low self-worth. We can be the one who calls another and says, "I have been thinking about you. How are you?"

Sometimes we need to act "as if." We need to say to ourselves, "How would a person with self-worth act? Act that way." Then, rather than hang back from interaction, afraid of intruding, we call the recent widow and offer our condolences, we call the flighty student and offer to meet for a cup of coffee. We act out of a sense of our own worthiness, and in doing so we reinforce the worthiness of others.

All creative acts require daring, and daring is something that can be learned. We dare, first of all, to accept ourselves as we are in the moment. We dare, next, to accept that that may be enough. Writing from where we are, painting from where we are, acting from where we are, we make beauty of the places we have been. By insisting to ourselves that beauty is present even on those days when we cannot see it, we make the beauty in the world more real. The fact that today I cannot see the mountains in my valley does not mean that they are gone. In the same way, the fact that some days we cannot see our own beauties does not mean that they are gone. It is worth instigating a line of gentle questioning.

If I felt I were beautiful enough, good enough, and worthy enough, how would I act?

Act that way.

REMEMBERING
WHO WE ARE

Try this: When we seek to have greater self-worth, we often ignore the word "self" in that equation. In order to have self-worth, we must ask ourselves what our true self appreciates. Acting in alignment with our true values is what brings us self-worth. Take pen in hand. Number from 1 to 10. List ten qualities or accomplishments that you appreciate about yourself. Complete the following phrases as rapidly as possible:

1. *Something I really appreciate about myself is*
   _____.

2. *Something I really appreciate about myself is*
   _____.

3. *Something I really appreciate about myself is*
   _____.

4. *Something I really appreciate about myself is*
   _____.

5. *Something I really appreciate about myself is*
   _____.

6. *Something I really appreciate about myself is*
    _____.

7. *Something I really appreciate about myself is*
    _____.

8. *Something I really appreciate about myself is*
    _____.

9. *Something I really appreciate about myself is*
    _____.

10. *Something I really appreciate about myself is*
    _____.

Taking Heart

TODAY I READ A BOOK that a friend of mine wrote. It took her two years to write it and it took me a day to read it. It was so good that I gulped it down. What I remember about the writing of the book was my friend's agony over whether the work was any good, the long silences she suffered through from her editor, and the long seasons of self-doubt that the silences triggered.

"Maybe I should just give up writing," I remember her thinking at one point. "Maybe after thirty years I have done enough of it and I am just too thin-skinned to keep it up. What's the point anyway? It's just a book."

It is ironic to me that the book my friend so despaired of may be one of the best she has ever written. It tells me how far off-kilter we can go that she didn't sense that, that she didn't somehow stubbornly stay her book's champion even in the endless months when it garnered no reception. Why couldn't she hold on to "It's good" or "I'm good"? But she could not—and furthermore, I understand why she could not, and I see this creative suffering all the time.

When we make something, we may love the process of making it, but we are also making it to serve a purpose, to connect to an audience and complete its life cycle. A silversmith makes a spoon to sip soup or to spoon trifle. When the soup is spooned, the trifle tasted, the silversmith can sigh, "Ah, that's good." A cycle stands completed. The artful article has found its appreciative audience. When we make a piece of art and no one samples it— or when they sample it without a little "mmm" of contentment, we suffer. We tell ourselves we should be more mature, that we should love our work just for our work's sake, but that sainthood eludes most of us. A piece of art needs a recipient. Otherwise we are pitching pennies down a well with no bottom. There is no tiny splash or "plunk" of connection, and so we feel lost, crazy, shallow, immature. But are we?

In our culture, the act of making art is removed from the dailiness of lives. Most writers are not like Dickens, writing his serialized page-turners to fill a Sunday supplement fueled by the appetite of his readers. Our art is marginalized. With the advent of television and the Internet, video games and computer games, most art is now relegated to a sidebar, an also-ran entry in the sweepstakes of life. A playwright is no longer writing to an audience that turns out to see plays as a way of life, a way to process national consciousness. Where once art was dead-center and art-making a calling that was embedded in the cultural life of a city, art-making now smacks of esoterica. Rather than being a primary way to process life, a summing up, art now is more diversionary. "He writes novels. . . ." (And who needs *them* anymore?)

When artists were simultaneously more revered and more ordinary, art was something that was rallied to and supported. Art preceded the entertainment industry. Books were exciting and central to our lives. The novelist was a sort of marathon hero. Ditto the painter, the sculptor, the dancer. They brought a beauty and specialness to life's experience. They created art as a distillate of the collective consciousness for which they were the uniquely qualified spokesmen. Ezra Pound called artists "the antennae of the race," and the race was tuned in to those antennae, eager to know what was being picked up, "where we are heading." Now the news at ten purports to tell us the same thing. The endless talk shows feature top-of-the-head opinions rather than the shaped pieces of consciousness that are created art. We have instant responses now to world events. Art takes time, and it is in this very taking of time that the artist is often worn down.

The book I read today—devoured today, it was that savory—was two years in the writing. Those were two years without feedback, lonely years of self-discipline, long hours at the keys, longer hours carrying the burden of the book's invisible weight. My friend is a successful writer, therefore a writer presumed to be beyond the humble need for encouragement. But none of us, really, is ever beyond that need. Like any other worker, we need the occasional pat, "Job well done." In art, such pats are few and far between. (When work becomes public, critics may wield brickbats, not pats on the back.) This is hard to deal with, and just how we do deal with it is something each of us works out for ourselves. Many of us, conscious of our neediness, try to build a life with ego structures in it other than work, so that if work is wobbly, we can still relate in terms of our other roles—wife, mother, lover, friend. Yet work is central, and most artists, ashamed of their need for encouragement, try to carry their work to term like a secret pregnancy.

"What are you up to these days?"

"Yes, well, I'm working on a book. . . ." The voice trails off. The tone says, "Let's drop it."

We artists have heard too many stories about the artist as spoiled brat, the artist as greedy egotist, for most of us to want to impose even a soupçon of this on our friends and colleagues. And so we bunker in with our projects, beleaguered by our loneliness and by the terrible secret that we carry: We need friends to our art. We need them as desperately as friends to our hearts. Our projects, after all, are our brainchildren, and what they crave is a loving extended family, a place where "How'd it go today?" can refer to a turn at the keys or the easel as easily as a turn in the teller's cage.

TAKING HEART

Try this: Art is an act of connection. We make
art in order to communicate. This means that
our eventual audience is important to us, and
is part of the life cycle of our work. Take pen
in hand and number from 1 to 5. Select five
people from your friends and acquaintances
who are good catcher's mitts for your creative
projects. Next to each name, describe the particular qualities that make that person a desir-
able audience member.

Now number from 1 to 5 again. This time
write the names of five people who should *not*
be allowed as early viewers of your work. Next
to each name, write why, and which qualities
lead you to exclude them. This is an exercise in
discernment.

Survival

IT HAS BEEN RAINING lightly in late afternoon, but the rains have been so slight that they have neither quenched the thirsty earth nor washed clear the atmosphere. A normal summer's night in New Mexico is spangled by stars. Constellations are flung, glittering, horizon to horizon. But now the smoky nights blot out the stars. Sleepers toss restlessly, breathing air still tinged by cinders. The hiking trails are closed due to fire hazard. Die-hard hikers complain, but they comply. The forests are empty of humankind. The glorious landscape is cloaked by a shroud—visitors can only be told about the azure bowls of sky that they are missing. One day at a time, the tainted skies can be tolerated, but only a day at a time.

Just as people can live and work under the smoke-choked sky, so, too, in a creative career we often pass through times of difficulty. There are periods when the time and solitude to work are in short supply. Other times, we have the time but lack the inspiration. It is in the patient moving-through of all forms of creative weather that we learn that we *can* move through them, and that we should. It is a question of perspective. "Just for today, I can handle this circumstance," we say as we drive uptown to run an errand and steal an hour alone in a café to do our writing. Art is like lovemaking; where the genuine ardor is there, the will *will* find a way. It is a piece of hard-won advice that if a man is too busy to call you, he is not in love. If we are too busy to make art, we are not artists. Artists, like all true lovers, steal moments from the crowded day. A half hour in the quiet house before the children wake, that stolen hour at the café, forty-five minutes before bedtime—these small increments of scrounged time add up to our commitment. Just as life goes on despite the smoke, art goes on despite the life.

We use the phrase "practicing artist," but we seldom allow ourselves to enjoy the nuance of meaning it conveys. We do not need to be perfect as artists. We do not need to create every day. But we do need to create *most* days. We do need to practice our creativity, wedging it in, however imperfectly, amid our busy activities. Because the part of us that creates is youthful and vulnerable, the making of art cannot be deferred too often or too long. Like a small child, our artist simply does not understand delays and denials. Like a small child, our artist is easily hurt, easily scarred by indifference and inconsideration.

Conversely, like a small child, our artist is easily bribed and encouraged. We can coax our artist into cooperation. We can cajole our artist into creation. Bribes work, and so does trickery. We can take our artist on writing or sketching dates, hoodwinking it through a little cheerful company into doing our will. The point, always, is to keep working, and to keep that work as close to play as possible. We can woo our artist like a lover, enticing it out to play with the small, festive expeditions I call Artist Dates. A movie may be good for our novelist. A bookstore may serve our painter. The highly colored bolts of silk in a fabric shop may lead us to more colorful art. Small steps, very small steps, lead to large

changes. A novel is written a page at a time. In a year, we can ac-
cumulate 365 pages at the modest rate of a page a day. A needle-
point project undertaken in snatched moments can come to fruition
within a month. Adversity may steal our hours and our attention,
but adversity, like smoke, can be survived.

SURVIVAL

Try this: As artists, we are hardy creatures. We survive adverse circumstances and prevail despite them. We seldom give ourselves credit for our own hardihood. Take pen in hand. Number from 1 to 5. List five difficult periods in which you managed to both survive and make art. For example:

1. *The year I had a crazy adviser for my thesis*
2. *The year my job demanded overtime*
3. *During my pregnancy*
4. *During my husband's illness*
5. *When I had young children underfoot*

Most of us lead lives embedded in busyness, and yet we manage to make the business of art-making a priority. We owe ourselves a vote of gratitude for our own survival.

Catalysts

THOSE WHO PROVOKE US into art do so by their interest and enthusiasm. They are curious about life. Curious about what we have to say about life. They themselves have not given up on life. They are interested in mysteries—interested in the mystery of what we will have to say. In a word, muses find us amusing. They smile at our jokes. They frown at the questions we raise. They are lively in response to our living art. When we drop a penny down the well of their consciousness, it makes a "splash" when it hits bottom.

People who catalyze us are not chilly and withholding. They tell us what they think—which may not be quite what we wish to hear. They say, "What do you mean by that? I am not quite clear." They say, "Do you mean this to apply in all cases?" People who catalyze us are responsive. They have nervous systems that react. They have minds that range with curiosity over the questions that we raise. They remember the questions we have raised before and they remind us when we have shifted our ground and our perspective. They act like we are interesting. They themselves are interested in life. They are not blasé. They do not feign boredom. They are not "too sophisticated" or "too intellectual" to get emotionally involved with the grit of living.

A muse has enthusiasm. During the season that I wrote my crime novel *The Dark Room,* I met my muse, Ellen Longo, for lunch every day at Dori's Café. Over a burrito or a bowl of red beans and rice, I would read Ellen the day's chapter, and she would "oooh" and "ahhh" at my hero Elliot's adventures. An accountant and an astrologer—not an unlikely combination in Taos—Ellen took an interest both in the details and the story lines of my characters' lives. She had a particular fondness for Dr. Violet Winters, Elliot's "love interest." Muses take interest in our creative process, recognizing the fact that making art is a risky and enlivening venture, and one that they feel privileged to get to share. A muse may be enigmatic but probably not—certainly not all the time. It is more than likely that Mona Lisa had a few opinions and shared them with da Vinci when he put down his brush.

A muse is a reflecting mirror that shows us "This is worth it." A muse acts as if life is adventurous, as though our grappling with the page or the canvas or the clay matters and has significance. Muses tell us we are not alone, that the bone we drag back to lay at their feet may be delicious and well worth the struggle. Think of Mona Lisa again, that sly, delighted, secretive smile. That is certainly worth provoking in someone. Our muses may grace us with smiles or with hoots of delight. They may scrawl on the edge of our manuscript, "Now, this is interesting!"

A muse has an appetite, and that appetite makes us hungry to express ourselves. A muse is never glutted on life, on too much thinking and too much input. The muse cocks an ear, cranes forward slightly, and lets us know that what we have yet to say and yet to think may be the most interesting of all the tidbits yet.

Those who dampen us act above it all. No matter how interesting our thoughts or conjectures, they seem to be barely stifling a yawn. Boredom is the pose they take most often. Cynicism is another favored guise. Cynics are monsters to the creative process.

They are poison and anathema to the impulse to make something. They act as if whatever we have in mind is somehow beneath them and that they are really slumming spending time with us and our interests.

"Oh, dear, is that all you have to say?" is the sentiment they seem to embody. And they embody it no matter how riveting our insight may actually be. Unlike the muse who takes a mysterious and even mischievous interest in our thoughts, the non-muse takes a callow indifference. Nothing is ever quite good enough to really merit the full focus of their haughty attention.

Not all muses speak to us with words. Sometimes a muse uses art itself to provoke us into artistry. I knew a flautist whose music was a positive Pied Piper to my storyteller. I would listen to him play and then want to play myself, but with words. A pianist proved another positive muse. His rippling melodies sent me running to both the piano and the page, striving to communicate something back in response to what I had heard. The Impressionists provoked paintings in one another. They were both friends and muses. But enemies can be muses as well, causing us to make art "right at them." A muse can be anyone, anyone who sets our creative engine humming. So we whistle while we work.

CATALYSTS

Try this: Another word for "muse" is "fuse lighter." Some people simply provoke us into art. We respond to their interest and enthusiasm as to a welcome challenge. Such people are invaluable. It is not that we would not make art without them, but we might make less art, or art of a lesser caliber. Number from 1 to 5. Allow yourself to cherish the fuse lighters you have known. List their names and the projects they sparked. If you are short on fuse lighters, you may need to seek some out. If you have lost touch with a pivotal fuse lighter, you may wish to reestablish contact. Do this by phone, letter, or e-mail. If you live in the same town, you may want to make a date for coffee or drinks.

Taking Care

THE CANYON THAT PLUNGES south from Taos to Española, the one that features so many hairpin turns, is studded by floral crosses marking the spots where drivers have miscalculated and plunged from road to river below. The crosses are beautiful and festive, and if you don't know what they mean, they are enjoyable. To the rest of us, they are a constant warning: Slow down, do not be arrogant. Do not be reckless. Take care.

Sometimes our creativity escalates. Ideas and images flow to us rapidly. We work with unusual ease and spontaneity. Barriers melt away; we are sailing. At times like these, when we experience flow rather than block, it is important to observe the warning signs, to recognize that danger as well as exhilaration lies in the hairpin turns we giddily execute.

When a piece of work is going well, we need to take special care of our creative stores. If we binge on our capacity to work, maniacally flying along our creative track, we run the risk of accident. Often I have had people say to me, "Julia, I don't understand. It was going so well, and now I'm blocked." I want to tell them, "Remember what I've said. You are blocked *because* it was going so well. You outstripped your creative stores. You have burnout." As a rule of thumb, when our work is going well and we are tempted to binge on it, instead we must double our Artist Dates, working consciously to replenish the stores we have overdrawn. When we are working well, our artist feels tireless, even superhuman. But we are the vehicle through which our art enters the world. If we are short on sleep, on healthy recreation, on genuine interaction with those we love—these lacks will impact our artist. This is why Henry Miller advised artists to gain interest in life, in the world around them. He well knew the dangers. The world is teeming with interesting things, Miller advised us. If we fail to enjoy this earth, blaming it on our art, our art will lack earthly vitality; like a hothouse tomato, it will be flat and forced. This is vital to remember. Artists whose work becomes too rarified, too inbred, and self-referential risk losing the very audience with whom they hope to connect. Great artists are great populists, for ideas are everywhere.

"Are you with me? Are you following me?" These are the questions we ask when we are speeding through an explanation. The same questions serve the artist at all times. Too much velocity, and we lose coherence. An idea may come to us in a flash, but it can take years to effectively execute what we so suddenly saw. When the idea of an opera about Magellan came to me, it came in a sudden flood of music and images. I raced to get them down on the page, terrified that I would lose what I saw—but then the flood passed, and for five more years I limped behind it, working patiently to capture what I had seen. I studied old maps and the diary of Magellan's comrade. I read various historians' writings on his heroic voyage. Little by little I allowed my imagination to live at sea, as Magellan had. This patience paid off in my work. Work that is forced to come through too quickly often lacks clarity and specificity. It takes time to fill in the details, time to find the right details to fill in. Above all, it takes a full image bank, not one that we have overused in our hurry.

TAKING CARE

Try this: When our work becomes too heady, we need to get grounded by moving back into our bodies. There are a variety of ways to do this: walking, eating, cleaning, napping. Many of us use a combination of these, but I would like to suggest another powerful alternative: mending. That's right, mending. Most of us have a few tattered things that could benefit from our time and attention. When we sew, we sow the seeds of our creative success. The action of sewing, like that of swimming or scrubbing, is regular and repetitive. Any regular, repetitive action moves us out of logic brain and into artist brain. There we encounter the solutions to our creative difficulties. To test this theory, try doing some mending, and observe how quickly you feel centered, grounded, and peaceful.

Rebirth

YESTERDAY IT RAINED. Great, heavy drops fell from the leaden sky. Lightning struck like jagged swords. Thunder rolled through Taos Valley. A high wind lashed the falling drops so they fell sideways in torrents on the windows of my old adobe house. Finally, joyfully, the so-long drought was at an end. Under the falling rain, the moistened sage gave off a heavy perfume. The piñon stands on the lower mountain slopes gave off a resinous fragrance. The earth once again felt rich and green. With every drop came the hope and promise of a renaissance.

Creative droughts end without the fanfare of thunder and lightning. One day it is hard to work, almost impossible. The next day it is easier. Our perfectionist has backed off enough for us to have some room. Just as the first rain happily signals an end to the drought, so, too, the first good day's work signals the beginning of a new ease. We have come through the hard times, and we are reaping the rewards of our gentle perseverance. Just as the rains wash away the accumulated dust and debris of a longstanding drought, so, too, a good day's work restores us to sanity and optimism. Once again we are able to feel our spiritual taproot. We can sense the forces of inspiration moving through us. We feel not alone but connected—once more in contact with the Great Creator and its intention for us to create.

Rain ends with rainbows, great colored arcs over Taos Valley.

Sometimes the rainbows are multiple, two and even three rib-
boned bands. If we could, we would send up a colored fanfare to
celebrate our own creative homecoming. We would signal our
exuberant hope with a sky-touching omen. Yet creative breakthroughs are more quietly colorful. One day we are able to make
the phone call that had us stymied. From out of nowhere we have
the power—or faith—to support our work. Droughts do end, and
so do periods of creative hardship. If we are faithful to our practice
of Morning Pages, Artist Dates, and Walks, droughts end sooner.
For what is a drought, really, but a prolonged period of doubt
when our faith wears thin?

Ellen, a writer, finds she cannot write easily. For months she
struggles uphill, straining to put words to the page. Faithful to her
practice of Morning Pages, she finds those pages filled with creative missives. She doubts she will ever write again, at least not
easily and with joy. And then, one afternoon, the impossible is
suddenly possible. She takes to the page lightly. Her pen has wings.
Giddy with relief, she is yet afraid to trust her newly rediscovered
powers. "It's just a freak," she tells herself, certain that the window
of creativity will slam shut again. Yet, faithfully, she writes, grateful for the grace she's been granted, grateful that for one day the
drought has eased.

Out of a sky half clouded and half clear, a moistening rain
begins to fall again. It is another blessing; the earth is still thirsty.
Authorities say fourteen more inches must fall before the govern-
ment forest lands will be reopened to summer hikers. Fourteen
inches of rain seems an impossible amount, a torrent. And yet it is
raining, and with every drop the parched land grows greener.

All artists suffer times of creative doubt—and drought. The

bogeyman of fear and self-criticism, the knife blade of perfection-ism, looms close to each of us. Blocks cannot be eliminated, but their ability to effectively block us can be. The trick to work is working, the gentle persistence to remain on the page, to show up at the easel or sketchpad. At our most dull and deadened, we are still often artful. Despite our moods, despite our self-flagellation, creativity moves through us; like our blood, it is an unseen river that supports our life.

REBIRTH

Try this: It is easier for many of us to focus on our defeats than on our victories. We seldom celebrate the many milestones that we could. Focused on product, we ignore the process of our art. This tool asks you to celebrate your life in process. Take pen in hand and complete the following phrase as rapidly as possible:

    1. If I let myself, I could celebrate
    ————————————.

    2. If I let myself, I could celebrate
    ————————————.

    3. If I let myself, I could celebrate
    ————————————.

    4. If I let myself, I could celebrate
    ————————————.

    5. If I let myself, I could celebrate
    ————————————.

A sense of celebration brings life joy and succulence. We are intended to enjoy the good things of this earth, including our own endeavors.

Resiliency

THE SUMMER RAINS HAVE COME. Taos Valley is restored to balance. The flocks of grazing sheep and herds of cattle once again nibble a tender green. The parched brown grasses, flattened low to the earth by dusty winds, create now a gentle shelter for the new growth brought by the rains. The giant pines found at higher altitudes no longer shed their needles like dull brown pins. Restoration is at hand. The earth is resilient.

As creative beings, we, too, are resilient. We are watered by the slightest daily practice that brings our creativity gently to bloom. Our Morning Pages, like moistening rain, keep our spirit from becoming parched and dry. Our Artist Dates, like a sudden drenching torrent, revivify our creative wellsprings. Even the shortest Walk restores sanity and a sense of scale. We are citizens of the green earth, attuned again to its tempo, finding in our own bodies the rhythm of the ages.

Alice, a sculptress, suffered through a long creative drought. She wrote her Pages daily, she took her Dates and Walks, and she waited out her inner censor's grim and unrelenting scorn.

"I am so grateful I was able to be stubborn," she laughs, "and stubborn is really what it boiled down to. I did my Pages no matter what. I *refused* to let my censor triumph. I told myself that even though I did not feel creative, I was creative. I repeated that over and over to myself, making it a kind of mantra. I needed something to drown out my censor's voice. I also had a sneaking suspicion that my block had appeared because I was on the verge of a breakthrough, not a breakdown."

Happily, Alice was correct in her suspicion that her block was a last desperate attempt at sabotage by her censor.

"I cannot tell you the fiendish cruelty my censor displayed to me," Alice recalls. "My every idea was 'terrible.' I was over the hill, dried up, done for, a has-been. Pretty much every fear that lurked in my subconscious was used by my censor in its attempt to disable me. I'm just grateful I had the courage to keep working somehow. My humor is part of what saved me."

It was Alice's humor that suggested to her that as long as she was "fishing for ideas," she might as well do some mobile sculptures with fish. Brightly colored, whimsical, and beautiful, these sculptures featured fish floating amid driftwood. Sometimes a sculpture held as many as thirty colorful fish. Sometimes as few as five, carefully chosen. What all of the sculptures had in common was their mischief and imaginative playfulness, a lightheartedness that Alice did not feel but nonetheless embodied in her art.

"I don't want to say that money is the bottom line, but when those sculptures began to sell despite my censor's criticism, I began to think, 'I'm onto something here,' and I was." From flying fish, Alice moved to mobiles of multicolored horses, flying in flocks. These, too, captured an immediate audience. "There's something to be said for sheer orneriness." Alice laughs. "I had enough years of creative recovery to have the faith to keep working despite my censor. In fact, I came up with a new theory: It's my belief that the nastier the block, the bigger the probable breakthrough."

Alice's story is not unusual, nor do I believe she's wrong in her theory regarding blocks. Time and again I have seen the finest work greeted by the most ruthless inner resistance. It is worth thinking of our inner censor as our inner saboteur. If we are bent on the successful accomplishment of our dreams, our censor is bent on keeping us small and dreamless. But we are not small and dreamless. We are large, we are powerful, we are resilient.

RESILIENCY

Try this: We are very strong, but we seldom credit ourselves with our strength. All lives contain great blows from which we must recover. We must recover, and we do recover. This is our resiliency. Take pen in hand. Number from 1 to 5. List five blows from which you have recovered. For example:

1. *The sudden death of my friend John*
2. *The loss of my job*
3. *A severe bout of depression*
4. *A bad car crash*
5. *Losing my friendship with Martha*

In each of these situations, we had to muster the inner strength to face life anew. We contain such strength at all times; it is our untapped inner resource. We can count on it: We are resilient.

Receptivity

FOR TWO DAYS the winds from the mountains have blown strong and harsh. Both rain and debris have been borne along by them. A large rain has saturated the earth, but now the wind demands another sort of submission, flattening the sage, bending the piñon trees, raising again clouds of dust, then pushing them to earth. Such wild winds are inconvenient and alarming. No house is snug enough to evade their prying fingers. On sideboards and bureaus, a fine coat of red-gold dust develops. Cyclists and hikers stay indoors. Gardens flatten to the earth. Nature rules.

When nature holds ascendance, acceptance is key. So, too, we must practice acceptance when in the grip of a large creative project. We do not really write a book, paint a picture, sculpt a sculpture, or dance a dance. In these and all art forms, something larger than ourselves works through us, and our openness and receptivity are key. Art holds mystery at its core. We can conceive a project and yet, like any conception, we are only participating in the inauguration of an independent life. Novelists tell stories of their characters' rebellion. Choreographers speak in awe of the new shapes and forms they are called to put into being. It is no different in the performing arts. When a pianist undertakes a composition, that composition bears its own life force, shaping the player as much as it is played. When we are engaged in the creative process, we are engaged with higher forces. Mysterious forms and forces seek entrance through us, and we had best cooperate.

For this reason, I often say that art is an act of the soul and not of the ego or intellect. To make great art requires great humility, the willingness to be obedient to what would be born through us. We are immersed in our creative projects. We are subject to them as to a great wind.

Art impregnates us. We carry its new life. Waking or sleeping. A project is not finished until it is born, and it is born on its own schedule, not our own. In the initial phases of a piece of work, we may retain the illusion of control. We set a steady schedule and work to that. As our creative gestation continues, the inner life gains more and more primacy. A large project may carry an imperious energy, demanding from us time and focus. Creative breakthroughs are exactly that: an onslaught of creative energies that override our set and conventional boundaries. Just as a strong wind demands entry into our houses, a piece of work may insist on occupying our psyche. We may be talking to our children, dining with a husband, visiting with a friend—but we do not do it alone. The work is always present, always working its way through us, working even when we are not working, changing shape and form to find its entry to the world. In all of this, our task is submission, not mastery.

When we agree to be an artist, we agree to open ourselves to art. An artistic career involves less the coercion of art into forms we dictate than our cooperation with the forms dictated by art itself. It is this agreement to shape-shift that brings to the artist a childlike vulnerability. Children are responsive to the moment.

THE SOUND OF PAPER

Their moods are quicksilver, changeable, fleeting. The artist, too, must possess this fruitful mutability. We are shaped by the shapes moving through us. It is our obedience to the winds of inspiration that makes the artist a contrary citizen. It is not that we *intend* to be unpredictable, rather, that we *tend* to obey the dictates of a creative urge. Sometimes one intimates greater tractability than we can honestly muster. As artists, we are sworn to openness. Like the sage, we must bend willingly to the wind.

RECEPTIVITY

Try this: Art is a collaborative process. Even when we practice a solo art form, we do so in collaboration with our universe. Many times our outer life impacts and colors our inner life. The two are interconnected. Take pen in hand. Number from 1 to 5. List five people, places, or situations that became a part of your artistic life. For example:

1. *Taos: the setting for my book* The Right to Write
2. *Mark Bryan: the catalyst for my book* The Artist's Way
3. *New York: the setting for my book* Walking in This World
4. *Tim Wheater: the catalyst for my play* Love in the DMZ
5. *Emma Lively: my catalyst and collaborator on the opera* Magellan

As artists, we are not immune to our surroundings, we are attuned to them. If we allow it, life can feed our art.

Courage

THE ROAD WEST FROM TAOS runs straight as an Indian's
part. It bisects sage fields stretching to the horizon on each side.
One hundred miles away lies a mountain range, but long before
that mountain range lies the gorge. Six hundred feet deep, one
quarter mile wide, it is the reminder of the Rio Grande's power to
cut through rock. The Rio still flows at gorge bottom, notching it
ever deeper. The gorge is an unexpected crack in the earth. A great
gaping wound amid the sage fields. Now a steel-girded bridge spans
its width. But to the early traveler, it was impassable, a sudden and
catastrophic tear in the map. To cross the gorge required a forty-mile
trip downriver to Pilar, where the river could be forged.

Making art is a vocation, a calling like the urge that pushed the
settlers west. Often we enter the vocation of artist without knowing what it will entail. We strike out, just as the settlers did,
encountering mountains and valleys, only to come upon the sudden, impassable gorge. And yet, with effort and the courage to
explore, the great gorge *was* passable. So, too, with effort and the
courage to explore, our creative dreams are possible.

Even in the lives of ordinary citizens working their day jobs,
nine to five, the calling to write, say, a novel or an opera or a film
script can loom sudden and threatening as the wound in the earth.
And yet, the wound in the earth is natural, and so is the making of
art. We cannot always turn to those around us for mirroring and

support. Sometimes we must seek the example of our larger tribe, reading the biography of an explorer who has gone before us. Composers can find comfort reading about composers, especially when an autobiography is available, like Richard Rodgers's. What we are after here is the experience, strength, and hope of other artists, a sort of verbal legacy that states: "It is possible."

Not only is it possible to make art, and large pieces of art, it is possible to make that art in the lives we already have. It is not necessary for the novelist to secure a cabin in Yosemite. A composer does not require a Steinway in a Paris atelier. Great music can be written in Libertyville, Illinois. A novel can be born in Council Bluffs. Art is made a moment at a time, a day at a time, and we can make room in life as we know it for the art we yearn to make. First we find time for Morning Pages. Morning Pages train our censor to stand aside. Released from the burden of perfectionism, we are free to create. Songs come to us, and short stories. Obedient to their shape and form, we scribe them down. A day at a time, our art is born, and we as artists are born through it. To be an artist requires no special trappings. Our passport is stamped by art itself. It is the making of art that makes an artist.

Just as the settlers pushed west with many days of uneventful travel to the sudden, heart-stopping detour, so, too, an artist's life unfolds with daily regularity and the occasional heart-stopping challenge. We are called to make art, and we are sometimes called to make specific pieces of art that seem far beyond our capacities. An opera wants to be born, or an epic historical drama. We doubt our abilities, but the calling is imperious and not to be denied. And so, feeling as crazy as Don Quixote tilting at windmills, we answer the call. In my own career, I have spent five years on an opera, seven years on a musical, several years on a play. Sometimes fifteen years have elapsed between the conception of a piece and its successful execution. To be an artist is to learn patience, the same patience settlers learned trekking toward the distant mountains a day at a time until one day the mountains were at hand.

COURAGE

Try this: Although we seldom acknowledge it, we are all courageous. It takes courage to undertake a creative project. It takes courage to sustain it and complete it. It takes courage to make art in the midst of everyday life. Making art a priority takes courage. Take pen in hand. Number from 1 to 5. List five ways in which you have been courageous for your art. For example:

1. *I have done Morning Pages daily for two decades*
2. *I have written many works for love, not money*
3. *I have completed multiple drafts of hard projects*
4. *I undertook piano at age fifty-four*
5. *I have reserved time from my teaching to make my art*

All of us can make lists such as the one above. We have all overcome adverse circumstances. Courage is a necessary ingredient of art.

As artists, we all have it.

Persistence

FROM TRES PIEDRAS TO TAOS falls a lunar landscape. The sage fields stretch in all directions, gray, green, and monstrous, the color of moon rock as seen on television when our astronauts landed. Barely breaking the earth, a fleet of "earth ships"—subterranean homes—stud the terrain. The vista is hallucinogenic—adobe houses shaped in fanciful spirals pierce the azure sky. Dirt roads bisect the highway. They are largely unmarked.

Sometimes, in the making of art, we pass through a trackless landscape. Our projects are large and our landmarks are few. Writing a novel may loom like driving cross-country: Here is the Mississippi, there are the Rockies, but what lies between? It takes faith to be an artist, the faith to forge forward when the horizon is cloud-obscured and indistinct. The artist's prayer could be this one: "Lord, I believe; help my disbelief." Agnes de Mille tells us: "An artist never knows quite where he is going. Instead, we take leap after leap in the dark."

Art is not often commissioned. We commission ourselves to make art. A young arranger works three years on a musical project that may or may not meet with a warm reception. A playwright wrestles with draft after draft, trying to bring to the stage the drama that unfurls in his mind. Artists love other artists, and part of what we love is their courage.

My good friend Natalie is halfway across a new book. She has published many books, a number of them under contract. But this book has been undertaken with no publishing commitment. It is being written in the hope of publication but not the guarantee. For a year now, Natalie has written into the void. The book requires perhaps another year, maybe more. Natalie puts hand to the page, writing longhand, steering her book through the netherworld of art in process. Just as the road from Tres Piedras vanishes into the distance, so, too, the final chapters of her book shimmer as a chimera, and yet she drives herself toward them. This is persistence.

After the signal success of his book *The Milagro Beanfield War,* novelist John Nichols wrote daily for a decade without seeing publication. The road to Tres Piedras is short by comparison with the span Nichols endured. It is the making of art, not our art "making it," that signifies an artist's life. Careers turn on a dime, artists are discovered "overnight," although seldom before they have passed through the dark night of the soul. Early settlers to the American West brought camels, knowing the dromedary was suited to long distances without water. An artist setting out must carry his own water, an inner belief that may not yet be mirrored by outer reality. In all artists there is a seed of inner knowing, a stubborn insistence in the face of doubt. It is this inner knowing that propels the artist across the harrowing reaches of hostile terrain common to making art.

PERSISTENCE

Try this: Faith is a commodity we always feel is lacking. Who among us feels he has "enough" faith? And yet, we all do. It takes faith to inaugurate a creative project. It takes faith to establish an atmosphere where our creativity can flourish. Take pen in hand and list five occasions in which you have demonstrated persistence.

For example:

1. *I went back to graduate school*
2. *I took an improv class*
3. *I hired an illustrator for my children's book*
4. *I submitted my short stories for publication*
5. *I made a CD of my garage rock band*

Joseph Campbell tells us that "when we follow our bliss, we are met by a thousand unseen helping hands." Take pen in hand. Number from 1 to 5. List five pairs of helping hands.

Encouragement

A SOFT RAIN FALLS in the late afternoon in hushed whispers, gently bathing the dusty sage. Taos Valley is parched after its long drought and drinks the drops in greedily. The hope is, if it rains hard enough and long enough, the air will be washed clean of the smoke from galloping wildfires, and the valley's sunburned grasses will green again, providing food for its grazing herds of sheep, cattle, and horses. It does not take much rain to revivify the valley and raise spirits. As this rain falls, high-tailed horses race across the Indian lands where they are pastured. They love the rain as much for its cooling their sunbaked hides as for the promise it holds of renewed food.

Rain is like encouragement. We need it, as artists, and the smallest amount can work wonders. At this time, a friend of mine is mid-stride on a new book. She e-mails it to me in chapters, knowing I am eager to read what she has written. I am her believing mirror, there to cheer her on even when her pitches are a little wild. I myself have enjoyed an excellent believing mirror in my friend writer Ed Towle. He has made his way through early drafts of my work, muttering encouragement and urging me to keep at it if a book was not yet in shape. Growing up, I did not have a believing mirror. As a young writer, I wrote a novel that no one in my family wanted to read. It sat, unmolested, on a living-room table. No one opened its virgin pages. We all need encouragement. We need those who can cheer on our process rather than merely applaud our finished product. An artist's life contains variable weather. Our moods may move up or down, depending on how well the work is going. A true believing mirror is someone who can reflect us back to ourselves, at any point in the process, as competent, capable, and gifted. Even one believing mirror doubles our faith in ourselves and renews our commitment to make art. Ideally, we have a cluster of believing mirrors, a number of strong friendships in which our work is seen and cherished. My friend Sonia Choquette, writer and psychic, often helps midwife my large pieces of work into the world. When I have doubt in my process, she will say, "But I see the book, and it's a good one." I think of Sonia's precognitive feedback as being a little like a creative sonogram. She is able to get a picture and report to me on the thriving health of a still-unborn piece of work. I have another friend, Larry, who takes a gleeful happiness in my successes— before they occur. Like Sonia, Larry enjoys a strong spiritual connection, and his faith in me and my work is palpable.

It may take some detective work to discover the believing mirrors in your life. It may take some trial and error as we divulge our secret dreams, first to those who doubt, and then to those who can believe. Belief has the same impact on a beleaguered artistic spirit as the welcome rain has on parched Taos Valley. Even the smallest amount of encouragement lifts our spirits. It is no accident that many novels contain dedications to loving spouses and the notation "without whose help, this book would not exist." I myself hold such a debt to Mark Bryan for his belief and support while I was writing *The Artist's Way*. It is always easy, in cozy retrospect after a large success, to see that a project *should* have been believed in, but when I wrote *The Artist's Way*, my then-agent thought it was a foolish project. "Who would want to read about creativity?" Mark stubbornly insisted the book was good and would find an audience. Of course, he was right.

Sometimes our believing mirrors are ephemeral. We may not have a human cheering section. We may take off in a new direction so strange to our friends that they cannot muster their belief in it. This is why we say creativity is a matter of faith. Sometimes our sole support for an endeavor is spiritual. I have even prayed to have my desire to write some work removed, only to have it strengthened. It is my belief that the Great Creator and spiritual forces larger than ourselves take an intense and immediate interest in our creativity. When we are willing to receive it, we are brought support bit by bit, piece by piece, just as we need it. We "stumble" on a tiny article. We "happen" to see a flyer. We overhear a conversation with needed information. We are led, guided, shown. It is fair play, however, to ask the universe for human support. As artists, we are like athletes. We often need a cheering bystander to make it across the finish line. This is not weakness; this is human nature. Art is an act of communication and connection. It is only natural that we harbor the desire to communicate and connect. One simple, well-timed compliment, like one rainfall, guarantees our continued growth.

ENCOURAGEMENT

Try this: Most of us have believing mirrors, those friends who have cheered us on during our creative endeavors. They may or may not be artists themselves. What they do value is our art, and the effort it takes to make it. Although we seldom acknowledge it, their encouragement can be pivotal in our productivity. Take pen in hand and number from 1 to 5. List five believing mirrors who have been your creative champions. From your list, select one name and write a thank-you note. You may wish to thank your entire list.

Milestones

T I N Y   A R R O Y O   S E C O is a postage stamp–size town, a colorful collection of craft shops, galleries, and family-run cantinas. On the Fourth of July it hosts a big parade—big for Arroyo Seco. There are tiny Indian dancers, mounted conquistadores, a posse of cowboys, a motley array of burros festooned with flowers, pulling carts. Because "Seco," as it is called, is also a home to Julia Roberts, the parade features Julia lookalikes waving gaily. On both sides of the tiny main street, crowds throng despite the fact that a young boy winds his way through them carrying a giant lizard and wiggling python. Sno-Kones are for sale for a dollar and ice cream cones for a dollar fifty. The crowd buzzes with neighborly cheer, taking enormous civic pride in the minuscule extravaganza. The festivities mark the Fourth as a genuine celebration, and the inhabitants of Seco welcome the special occasion to party.

A creative career can go a very long time without any genuine markers to celebrate. A novel may be five years in the writing, a musical may run seven, an opera nine. This is too long to go between start and finish. Milestones need to be noted and celebrated. A novelist I know celebrates her recurring character's birthday. A screenwriter marks each successive draft with a dinner for friends. A composer spends time and money to record each stage; select friends receive CD samplers celebrating progress. Like the tiny Seco parade, such markers are arbitrary and festive inventions.

As creative artists, we inhabit two worlds: the ordinary world we live in, and the extraordinary world of our creations. As any novelist will tell you, characters are as particular and ornery as everyday people. We come to know them as well as our friends. This morning, over a breakfast of bacon and eggs at the Dragonfly Café, I was startled to look up and see my detective hero, Elliot Mayo, looming in the doorway. Of course it wasn't really Elliot, but Bradford Reed, a local architect. Elliot's double in many ways, Reed holds a special place in my affections, just as Elliot does in my imagination. For those who live with us, our invisible cast of characters can be a threatening shadow world. Our intimates sometimes sense that our attention is often spoken for, that we are listening to a conversation or plot unspooling in our ears. In a sense, our artistic creations are like invisible playmates, unheard and unseen by others but very real to ourselves. My daughter grew up in a world peopled by my literary creations. She knew that Elliot had a claim on my time and affections just as a sibling would.

By celebrating the benchmarks of our creative passage, we give others a gentle entrée into our creative world. "Have lunch with me to celebrate this draft of my play," we might say, or "I'm going to the theater to celebrate having completed a series of paintings." Most of our friends would like to be friendly to our work, if they only knew how. We can make them privy to the details of our work's maturing, if not the details of the work itself. "I finished a hard chapter; let's go to the Rio Grande and swim," I might say to my friend Natalie. She doesn't need to read the chapter to understand the sense of accomplishment. Some of our work may receive public recognition. Other work, equally valid, may not. It is too easy to judge our work by its public validation. There is much more to a creative career than public success or failure. Our creations are our brainchildren, and like all children, they love a special occasion. A book that is cherished in its unfolding remains a happy memory. "Remember when I mailed it off to my agent and we went for Thai food?" Like the little Seco Independence Day parade, it doesn't take much to have a good time. The part of us that creates is vulnerable and childlike. Is it any wonder our artist enjoys a little hoopla? I don't think so.

MILESTONES

Try this: We often remark that the part of us that creates is young and vulnerable. We sometimes call our inner creator our "creative child." And yet we seldom focus on that child in a way that a child might appreciate. Select one, or a group of friends, and invite them to attend a dinner in honor of your inner artist. Explain to each guest that the dinner is your attempt to honor your artist for work well done. You may find that throwing an artist party inspires you to mark other creative milestones: finishing a first or second draft, submitting your work, starting a rewrite. Any of these occasions deserves respect and celebration.

Keeping Our Footing

TEN MILES NORTH of Taos lies the tiny town of Arroyo Hondo. As its name suggests, the little village straddles an arroyo, a gash in the earth. If you turn left just after Herb's Lounge, you are heading west toward the Rio Grande gorge. The paved road dwindles to gravel and then to dirt, twisting switchback upon switchback as it descends one thousand feet into the earth. As the road zigzags down the side of the gorge, willows rise up to meet it. Where there are willows, there is water, and soon the dark green Rio, with its silver ripples, is in view. The road meets the river at John Dunn Bridge, named for an early trader. The bridge is a modest affair, slippery and treacherous during rain or snow. Beneath the bridge, the swift-flowing river widens into a placid pool, deep and emerald. It is here that people swim, sunning themselves like lizards on the gray river rocks. A day at a time, a drop at a time, the river has carved the great gorge. Now it runs along the gorge bottom, innocently green and silver, its fierce, eroding current noticeable only when the waters are braved for swimming or trout fishing. So fierce is the flow, it can be difficult to keep your footing on the slippery riverbed.

When we are engaged in a large creative work, it can be difficult to keep our balance. We, too, can be swept away by the force of what is moving through us. It is for this reason that as artists we must take care to be self-protective. A novel or symphony, a photographic series or musical, all have an undertow. It can be tempting to surrender to this turbulent inner life and allow ourselves to be washed downriver. It is wiser to keep our footing, to keep the structure of daily life, the company of friends, and the diversion of hobbies. Keeping our grid in place allows us to make art a priority while still retaining a sense of perspective. Like the Rio, art is powerful even in its most quiet mode. Legends abound of artists' tumult in the creative rapids. It is for this reason we fear the power of our creativity. We have heard too many tales of creativity gone awry, of artists pushed to the brink of madness.

Creativity is energy. Energy can be safely grounded, asked to flow within our lives and within the boundaries we have set for it. Creativity can be as marvelous as electricity, illuminating the darkness around us. How do we ground our creativeness, and why do we ground it? Let's begin with the why. We are out to accomplish a *body* of work, not merely one piece. This means we must take the long view. Just as a marathon runner considers his running career as a whole, training and pacing himself accordingly, so we must approach our art at a temperate rate. Hemingway wrote five hundred words a day. He stopped when he was ahead, when he knew where he would pick up the next morning. His work as a writer was work to him. He was punctual, and, until his alcoholism got in the way, he was prolific. T. S. Eliot worked in a bank. Virginia Woolf ran a printing press. Raymond Chandler sold insurance. William Carlos Williams was a doctor. None of these day jobs interfered with the making of art. Rather, they gave structure and richness to their artists' lives. A wise artist is a temperate one, refusing to succumb to the temptation to binge creatively.

It is the slow, steady output of work that amasses into a body of work. Just as the Rio created that gorge a rivulet at a time, so, too, we make novels a page at a time. Very often, when we say, "I would love to undertake X, if only I had the time," we are imagining a blissfully distractionless epoch in which we are free to simply create. Experience shows, however, that such freedom is actually not freedom at all. Artists thrive on structure. Given too much time and space, our consciousness flows across the floodplain like a river overrunning its banks. Most writers cannot write all day. Most painters find they have only a few highly productive hours. Setting up a creative grid that allots time for family and recreation as well as work ensures that we will have the richness of temperament to execute rich work.

KEEPING
OUR FOOTING

Try this: In order for our artist to thrive, it requires careful grounding. The Brontë sisters had their needlework, T. S. Eliot had his daily job at the bank. Virginia Woolf ran a printing press with her husband, Leonard. Each of these artists remained carefully in touch with the current of daily life. All of us know certain activities that bring us relief and grounding. Take pen in hand. Number from 1 to 10. List ten activities, from mending to laundry to the making of fudge, that you find grounding. Select and execute one grounding activity. If you are in the throes of a creative project and working "full tilt," select and execute two or more activities.

The Artists' Tribe

TAOS IS AN AGRARIAN VALLEY. Three cultures coexist within its mountainous arms. First are the Native Americans, perched lightly on the land; their pueblo is the oldest continuously inhabited dwelling on the continent of North America. Native American lands are given over to horses and cattle. They are typically not irrigated. There is little need. For thousands of years, the land has done well without such tamings. Second, Hispanic culture, which for three centuries now has made the valley its home. Land-proud and prone to agriculture, the Hispanics built an irrigation system made from acequias—ditches—that crisscross the valley floor. With the Hispanic influence came sheep, orchards, cultivated fields, and gardens. Finally, the Anglos discovered Taos one hundred fifty years ago, coming first as traders and later as an influx of artists, drawn by the light.

For the most part, the three cultures coexist harmoniously, or perhaps, I should say, coexist with guarded rigidity. As the poorest, the Native Americans also consider themselves the purest. Intermarriage is frowned upon, and Native Americans largely keep to themselves. Like their reservation, they are open only so far. Hispanics, too, consider it "slumming" to date an Anglo. Where the Hispanics built gracious low-lying adobe homes, carefully barbered and tended, the Anglos have built homes that intrude on the landscape. Odd-angled and ungainly, sometimes made from tires,

Coke bottles, and other recycled commodities, the Anglo homes often resemble the UFOs said to frequent New Mexico.

As artists, we live as a separate culture, embedded in the America of the mass media but separate from it. For us, the paycheck is not what says "Job well done." The power to buy is not what constitutes our power. Our worth is not quantified in fiscal terms. As artists, we are engaged in the process of self-actualization, and it is our success or failure at producing a body of work that determines our stature. The greater American society teaches us to believe that money is what matters. As artists, we find value in beauty instead. A single poppy, fiery orange with a black center; a cactus, its hot-pink flowers pinched hard and dry by the drought; a stand of Russian olives glinting silver in the light; the dark power of the Rio Grande, its shores studded by flower-bedizened crosses marking the spots where lives were lost. These sights bring richness to our lives. These sights enrich our art. Thirty miles south of Taos, the tiny town of Velarde is synonymous with good fruit. Apples, apricots, and cherries are the crops there, and yes, they are delicious. As artists, we must have an appetite for life. We must partner with life's abundance. Living side by side with a culture that tells us our worth is our net worth, we must hold to a different standard, knowing in our bones that as we embrace life, life embraces us.

Ours is the first generation to have our concepts of artists brought to us by the press, and the press is focused on money. We read of actors' astronomical salaries, their huge homes, square footage included, and their conspicuous consumption of cars and clothes. The media eye is trained on the trappings of celebrity. In the pages of *People* magazine, we do not visit just any screenwriter, we visit Joe Eszterhas in the wake of his three-million-dollar script sale. We read of Demi Moore, not for her acting talent, but for her high-flying lifestyle, the coterie of assistants required by her and her former husband, Bruce Willis. Everything and everyone boils down to money. And in this financial focus, art and artistry are lost. As artists, we live within the society depicted, but we live apart from it as well. Unlike our culture, we cannot fixate on price tag or finished product. To do so is to deny ourselves the dignity of process. Just as the inhabitants of Taos Valley are charged with husbanding the lands in their care, so, too, we are charged with husbanding our lives. Too much drama, too little sleep, too great an emphasis on "things," and we lose our capacity to savor the sweetness of the everyday. We must strive to live within our culture, much as the inhabitants of Taos Valley do, noting our similarities but able to live differently.

THE ARTISTS'
TRIBE

Try this: Many of us have secret talismans that
symbolize to us our freedom from, or within,
convention. A woman writer I know always
wears red lingerie: No one sees it, but she
knows it's there. A portrait artist cherishes a set
of red long johns. She wears them on cold days
in the studio. A quilter believes yellow is the
color of creativity, and the room where she
works on her crafts is a sunny yellow-gold. Our
artist needs and deserves our acknowledgment.
There must be some secret festive and private
signal of its importance. Make yourself an artist's altar. A window ledge or bookcase shelf is
space enough. The important part is that it be
consecrated to your artist and contain items and
totems that speak to your creative imagination.

Odd Couples

My household includes two Arabian horses, Jack Merlin and Beethoven. Jack is a showy chestnut with a blaze and four white stockings and a flaxen mane and tail. At eighteen years of age, he looks eight, handsome and full of himself, a real playboy. "Jack likes to be the center of attention," a trainer once observed. "He's a ham." By contrast, Beethoven, named for his dark, prominent eyes, is a shy, retiring gray. Where Jack seeks attention, Beethoven avoids it, preferring to watch quietly from the corner of his stall. An odd pair, they are quietly compatible, trotting out together into the New Mexico sunlight, coats glistening.

Jack has been in my family for many years now. At the moment he belongs to Emma Lively, my musical collaborator, a young rider whom Jack is teaching. Beethoven joined the family just last summer, plucked from a roadside pen under a purple-lettered sign: "Horses for sale." If it works well to have matched Jack, an experienced horse, with an inexperienced rider, it works equally well to match Beethoven, an inexperienced horse, with a veteran. Today was a schooling day: walk, trot, canter, reverse, walk, serpentine, halt. For Emma and for Beethoven it is all new, all fresh and exciting. For me and Jack it is old hat.

Artists love other artists, and odd-couple pairings, young with old, are common. For the older artist, the young protégé is a glimpse in the rearview mirror. For the younger artist, the grizzled veteran holds the promise of the future. Linked by their love of art and their love of each other, Stieglitz and Georgia O'Keeffe were one such pair, Georgia O'Keeffe and Juan Hamilton another.

Artists are often great teachers. Through the centuries, artists have routinely apprenticed other artists. We do it still, often within the university system, in creative writing programs. An older artist shares experience, strength, and hope. A younger artist brings enthusiasm, ardor, and stamina. The combination is unbeatable. When I was in film school, my mentor was Jack Whitehead, an aged Hitchcock cinematographer. In my forties, my theatrical mentor was John Newland, then in his seventies. From both these men I learned artistic standards and the value of the Nike slogan "Just do it." For many artists, mentors are found in books. Biographies are valuable; autobiographies are invaluable. It is wonderful to learn straight from the horse's mouth, just as Jack teaches young Beethoven trail manners. Very often, as I watch Jack proudly carry Emma around the ring, I am reminded of John Newland and the pride he took in showing me the ropes.

Artists are generous with other artists, but a part of that generosity is enlightened self-interest. When we share our enthusiasms, they grow stronger. A painter talking to a painter about the painting life reinforces the idea that such a life is possible and positive. Rilke wrote his *Letters to a Young Poet* because, as Italo Calvino tells us, "the ear calls forth the story." We do not know how much we have to share, how much we have learned—and earned—until we are asked to share it. It is a simple pleasure, teaching. As artists, it comes to us naturally. After all, what is art itself but the naming of our experience? What does art do? Certainly, it teaches. Twelve-step programs often warn, "You have to give it away to keep it." And certainly, the act of giving away our knowledge makes it again fresh in our mind. I often joke, only half kidding, that I teach creative unblocking in order to stay unblocked myself.

The ride is over. Jack and Beethoven are unsaddled, and sweaty enough to merit a quick shower. As the elder, Jack goes first, modeling for the younger horse how to stay still, snorting, as the icy spray needles his hide. Beethoven watches, round-eyed. "Surely I can't be expected to behave through *that*," his manner says. And yet, when it is his turn, he stays still, snorting, imitating Jack, looking to the older horse for reassurance and encouragement.

ODD COUPLES

Try this: Artists have long apprenticed other artists. The sharing of a veteran artist's experience, strength, and hope is how we pass on our spiritual lineage. Most of us have made the acquaintance of one or more younger artists who deserve our encouragement and mentoring. Again, "You have to give it away to keep it," and the same may be said of our creative excitement and enthusiasm. Take phone in hand. Contact one deserving artist for a coffee date. You may wish to schedule such dates at regular intervals. I meet with one younger artist every week.

Containment

IN EARLY MORNING, the dirt roads of northern New Mexico are bordered by clear blue bursts of chicory. A romantic blue, a lavender blue, chicory blooms bravely in the cool morning air, and by midafternoon, when the sky is a blue anvil pulsing with heat, the chicory has folded its blossoms like tiny praying hands and closed in upon itself. We can all take a creative lesson from its containment.

It is well and good to say we should be strong enough as artists to withstand the blistering heat of criticism. In my experience, artists *are* strong, but, like the chicory, we are also delicate. At the height of his career, John Steinbeck won the Nobel Prize for Literature. He had given us such classics as *Cannery Row* and *The Grapes of Wrath*. Surely his stature as a brilliant novelist would seem assured, and yet, days after his Nobel ceremony, *The New York Times* ran a scathing critique suggesting he did not deserve the lofty prize. A man at the height of his creative powers, Steinbeck was unable to shrug it off. In fact, he was unable even over time to recuperate from the blow. In the three decades remaining of his life, he never wrote fiction again.

"Writers are delicate," clucks famed writing teacher Natalie Goldberg. I would say all artists are. Like the chicory, we are deep-rooted but shy, unable to easily withstand the blazing glare of publicity. The wise artist is the artist who has developed stratagems for public periods. Filmmaker George Lucas would open a film and promptly retreat to Hawaii, beyond the glare of the media. For most artists, in order to withstand publicity, a well-rooted before, during, and after life is a necessity. Our friendships must encompass those who understand that both success and failure bring burdens. A hostile review can provoke feelings of "Who did I think I was? Who was I kidding?" A glowing review can provoke remarkably similar feelings. "It was just a fluke, I'm just fooling everybody. They'll find me out sooner or later." We cannot afford to have an identity moored solely in our press persona.

American culture tends to think of fame as the great panacea. It is widely assumed that famous people are beyond ordinary human pain. For this reason, few people can empathize with the deep pain caused by a bad review. "At least they're writing about you," the thinking goes. It is widely assumed that what they write matters less than that they write. By the same token, a review that praises an artist to the stratosphere may be perceived not as fear-inducing but as ego-inducing. Well-meaning friends may even decide to "take us down a few notches, for our own good." These friends do not understand what Goldberg calls our "delicacy." This lack of understanding cost us decades of Steinbeck's work. What might he have produced if he had not been frightened out of the game?

Make no mistake: As art in America has become a commercial concern, fame in America has become a high-risk celebrity sweepstakes. A known artist is a brand name and is always on public display. For this reason, our private lives must be kept private and deeply nurturing. We cannot afford friends who will use our fame against us, dining out on the intimate details of our life. Like the chicory that dozes in the glare of the hot sun, our friends must learn to practice "zip the lip" when pressed for gossip. Whether our fame comes from a school play we've produced or a nationally distributed, well-reviewed film, the glare of the spotlight is unsettling. We may react like the thistle, loud and showy in our defensive posturing. We may react like the chicory, silent and withdrawn. The one thing that is certain is that react we will, because we are delicate and sensitive to changes in our environment.

CONTAINMENT

Try this: In order for us to practice containment, most of us have to *practice* it. Artists are
openhearted, and discretion is not our first
instinct. Take a blank sheet of paper. Draw a
medium-size circle. Inside that circle, place the
topics and projects around which you must
practice a protective discretion. Also inside that
circle, place the names of those chosen and
trustworthy few with whom you can share
your most fragile brainchildren. Outside the
circle, place the names of those with whom you
must practice containment and vigilance.

Waiting for Fame

DEEP BLUE-GRAY CLOUDS gather on the horizon. The mountains bulk black clouds against them. Slate streamers reach from the clouds to the earth—a distant rain. It is one of the idiosyncrasies of Taos Valley that it may rain to the north and stay dry as a bone to the south, or rain to the south and stay dry to the north. All eyes are trained to the horizon, hoping, always hoping, the rain will visit *here.*

In a creative career, waiting for fame to hit is like waiting for rain in a drought. It keeps us squinting toward the horizon, jealous of our luckier neighbors and dissatisfied with our own condition. Our culture invites us to think of art in terms of product, and one of the by-products of the "product" we produce is fame. Fame is different from recognition for a job well done. Fame is like empty calories—there's no nutrition in it. Our culture encourages an addiction to fame. Fame is marketed as a cure-all. We are taught by the media to believe that once we are famous, our lives will be blessed. A quick glimpse at the tabloids is all that is required to disabuse us of this notion. Clearly, the rich and famous are beset by human woes as much as we are, and added to those woes are the woes of being rich and famous. When we are focused on fame instead of on our work, we begin to ask the wrong questions. "Will this be my breakthrough project?" we ask, instead of "Is this project worthy?"

Alicia, a young actress, has made four films in the past year. Her work, good to begin with, has steadily improved, and yet she is dissatisfied. Her roles have made her well respected but not yet famous. And famous is what she is after. "Is this a smart career move?" actors like Alicia begin to ask themselves each time they are presented with a role. By definition, the smart career move is the one that makes them famous, and then, once they are famous, the smart career move is the one that keeps them famous.

Afraid of making the wrong move, afraid of aligning themselves with the wrong projects, many talented actors go for long stretches without working. It is not that they are not offered work, it is that none of the work offered them seems quite "right."

A hot novelist embarking on writing a second novel faces the same dilemma. Instead of writing another book, he or she must write the "right" book, the one that will keep fame intact. It is no coincidence that our most famous TV/film reviewer, Roger Ebert, uses thumbs-up or thumbs-down to indicate the worth of a piece of art. It is the same shorthand used to condemn or spare Christian martyrs at the Colosseum. Make no mistake, the public practice of art in our culture is a high-risk endeavor. A bad or unfair *New York Times* review—as I once had—and an artist can feel like leaving the country. Like John Steinbeck, we may remain public but undergo the private hell of self-doubt and self-flagellation. The wise artist makes provisions to survive the reviewing process. Director Hal Prince defensively schedules a first meeting on a new project for the day after opening a show.

Not all artists will lead public lives. Many of us as talented as those whom fame strikes may toil out our days in relative anonymity. For this reason, too, fame must be seen as capricious and different from respect.

In Taos Valley, the rain is moving north to south. It is accompanied by bold and sudden lightning strikes. Trees are split top to bottom, and this, too, is a lesson in what sudden fame can do to an artist's life. When an artist becomes very hot, it is easy to burn out. And, too, much that is precious may be incinerated from sheer proximity. It may not be that movie people are shallow and unable to make commitments. It may just be that fame is so difficult, few relationships can successfully contain it. The lightning strikes can set forest fires that burn destructively despite the rain. So, too, can fame rage through a life.

Try this: The best antidote to the fame drug is a healthy dose of self-worth. Look at that phrase "self-worth." It tells us that our value must be determined by ourselves alone. What follows is an exercise in self-worth. Take pen in hand and number from 1 to 50. List fifty separate things for which you can value yourself.

For example:

1. *I taught Domenica how to ride when she was just a toddler*
2. *I helped my friend Martha through a financial fiasco*
3. *I wrote, directed, and produced a feature film*
4. *I did a poetry album*
5. *I functioned as editor on a friend's creative project*
6. *I beat up the class bully*
7. *I nursed Hot-Note's sore hoof*
8. *I wrote to Bob regularly*
9. *I wrote to my father regularly*
10. *I grew good tomatoes*

Our list of worthy accomplishments will differ from person to person. Take pen in hand and write for fifteen minutes about what your list has taught you regarding your values.

Creative Cloudbursts

THE SKY IS MOLTEN SILVER. Some clouds are pewter, others as soft as sterling. Above Taos Mountain, the gray darkens to black. This is a big rain coming in. A crack of thunder, a bolt of lightning so bold and exaggerated, it looks cartooned. There is a high shriek as the bolt hits home and a tree is sheared in half. The air sizzles with electricity. Another rumble, a roar so deep-throated it seems to issue from the mountain itself, another crack, another bolt of lightning, and then the drenching rains. The drops fall like nickels, as though with a rain this big, even the droplets are outsize. As water hits the piñon trees, they emit a pungent, piercing perfume. Like the sage fields, they seem at their very best when drenched with rain and giving off their heady scent. Rain in Taos Valley is intoxicating, not only because of the recent drought, but by its very nature.

Clouds walk the earth, mountains play peek-a-boo behind their gauzy shawls. The rain itself, liquid silver, glistens in the branches and turns the hilly red dirt roads into wild-running creeks. People go a little crazy during a Taos storm. You'll see them splashing in the puddles like children, spinning like dervishes, laughing and catching each other by the hands. Magic is afoot, and many Taos denizens who moved to the tiny town for magic feel their faith reaffirmed. There is at once a great wildness and a great gentleness. It is like a love affair.

If most creativity has a calm daily quality, with practice fitting comfortably into our quotidian lives, there are some stretches of creativity that do contain the sudden heady drama of a mountain storm. We experience this amped-up voltage very much like a storm. The very onset of a project may come as a sudden torrential outburst, image after image, thought after thought, crashing into our consciousness with velocity and force. Sometimes the velocity lasts long enough that an entire rough draft gets completed. Other times, the initial voltage fades, leaving us to labor for years to bring in what we saw in that flash of inspiration. A project may move along routinely, only to suddenly pick up speed and intensity as we enter the homestretch. Suddenly the book, the painting, the film, is a downhill slalom that finds us struggling to keep our feet as we make the gates. The power of our creative forces can be frightening. It helps to remember that like the sudden storm, the energy will spend itself and freshly washed normalcy will return.

Seasoned artists develop strategies for coping with the strong bursts of creative energy as they come. One such strategy is Morning Pages. The pages keep us tethered to our daily life, grounded in the needs we have for current actions. "Call the bank. Call my sister. Remember to buy dog food. Remember to get Windex." Details are grounding, and so are duties. Canny artists know that it is best to stay grounded in the flow of daily life even during a riptide of creative activity.

Veteran artists come to recognize the symptoms of a creative surge. There is a quickening, like the scent in the air just before a storm. This quickening is a warning, and the wise artist passes it along. "I think I'm going to be pretty absorbed for a while," they learn to warn family and friends. "I'm just at that stage." Forewarned family and friends cope better with an artist's storm of self-absorption. "It's not that I don't love you," we need to say, "it's just that right now my work has my attention." The wise artist doesn't sever ties completely. He simply asks for a longer leash. "Can I tap base with you later? Could we talk on the phone? Can I give you a call when I'm through this?" A web of loose connections serves us, allowing us to keep our bearings as the creative compass spins. Certain friends are true north for us; the steadiness of their voice, even at a remove of a thousand miles, brings us to ourselves. These are friends who can function like ground control, eager to hear our flight plan and trajectory. It takes time to discover such friendships, to learn who among our acquaintances can withstand a bout of turbulence without fear. Our communication is often the key. We need to send up warnings—"Going down the rabbit hole; I'll be back as soon as I can."

For those who love us, such intense visitations by the muse can feel a little like we have run off to have an affair. Our understanding this and our vocal appreciation for their understanding this can go a long way toward easing troubled waters.

Just as the world is washed fresh after a sudden storm, so, too, can our regular life appear to glisten with wonder after the squall of a creative surge has passed. Our spouse, our children, the dog— who could ask for better companions? Gratitude seizes the heart as dailiness is restored. All that remains to remind us of the sudden storm is the deep quiet once it is over.

CREATIVE
CLOUDBURSTS

Try this: When we are in a creative cloudburst, we need to take special care to nurture ourselves, but often we do not know quite how. Take a blank sheet of paper. Once again, draw a circle. Divide it into six wedges. Label them as follows: sleep, nutrition, creativity, spontaneity, service, recreation. Place a dot in each wedge indicating how well you care for yourself. The outer rim is very well, the inner area is not well at all. Connect the dots. Is your self-care a healthy mandala? Or is it a jagged shellburst? In what areas do you need the most improvement? How can you give yourself that growth?

Creative Weather

AFTER A DRENCHING RAIN, water runs in small rivers along the border to the Native American lands. The sage is wet and fragrant; the sky features snowy thunderheads and clear patches of blue. Tranquility reigns as the valley, refreshed and washed clean, settles into a long twilight. Creativity has seasons and weather. A good day's work, like a drenching rain, leaves us washed clean and refreshed. There are corners of the artist's mind that are swept clean only by working. It is working that brushes away the cobwebs. It is working that unclutters the furniture and hangs the clothes in a more orderly fashion. It would seem that working takes energy, but often, a good day's work brings energy as we turn to our neglected chores with a fresh eye and new enthusiasm. Many therapists would be quick to tell you that artists are complicated beings driven by complexes and neuroses. I think that may be true—of *blocked* artists. But not for an artist who is working freely. That artist tends to be happy and user-friendly.

What does it take to work freely? First of all, it takes the gift of proportion. When an artist is able to see himself as part of a larger whole that works through him, a great deal of stifling ego is siphoned away. It is no coincidence that much great art was created in a spirit of service. To God, to the why, to the patron, or to a higher cause. Anything larger and grander than the self draws us to scale, allowing us a useful humility. The tiny town of Taos is dominated by its views of Taos Mountain looming visibly over the community. The beauty of the mountain, the day's weather wreathing the mountain—these are constant reminders that our lives are led in relation to a Great Creator capable of infinite magnitude and grandeur. The Great Creator works through us as we create. To the degree that we are able to conceive of our creating as a form of listening to what would be created through us, we are granted freedom.

When we are working well, it is always tempting to take credit for the work. "I am so brilliant!" we want to say. But if we do, we then put ourselves in a position of judgment rather than neutrality. One day, we will not seem brilliant. One day, striving to be brilliant, work will be difficult. One day, exhausted from striving, work will be impossible. When we allow work to work through us without the ego's constant judgment, we often produce work of a steady caliber. We are less bedeviled by the ego's ups and downs. We are less affected by mood. If it is our job to take care of the quantity and God's job to take care of the quality, then we can produce our work more readily, the way an apprentice chef serves a master chef, preparing the vegetables without knowing the full recipe.

It can be said that our talents are gifts from God and our use of our talents is our gift back to God. The degree of happiness we experience when working well, the sense of rightness and harmony, all argue that creativity is God's will for us. When we create, we work hand in glove with the Great Creator. Creativity is its nature and our own. We think—and manifest—from the mind of God within us. Artists throughout the centuries have known this and said this. They are not speaking in metaphor. Ours is one of the few world cultures that does not routinely honor higher forces, and yet, working at our art, we do experience inspiration, although we may call it an intuitive hunch or leading. Something within us leads, and we follow. Painter Robert Motherwell speaks of the brushstroke taking the next brushstroke. All artists experience this form of leading when our ego has stepped aside and we follow our inner muse with a childlike innocence and enthusiasm. Time falls away. We spend hours at the easel or the page, and time seems to pass in minutes. We have entered another, spiritual dimension. With our ego set aside, we lose our sense of separation from the source. We experience a time of communion, a conscious contact with a power greater than ourselves. We have touched the Great Creator, experiencing it as a power within ourselves. Is it any wonder that artists emerge, fresh as the valley after rainfall, from a sustained period of work?

CREATIVE
WEATHER

Try this: During a sustained period of work, artists require special care. We must be vigilant to not abuse our health and well-being. We must actively nurture ourselves. For each of us, the act of nurturing differs. Take pen in hand. Number from 1 to 10. List ten concrete ways in which you can support your artist during a season of hard work. For example:

1. *Go to bed an hour early*
2. *Stay in touch with close friends*
3. *Buy good groceries*
4. *Cook real meals*
5. *Continue to write Morning Pages*
6. *Double your number of Artist Dates*
7. *Continue to take Walks*
8. *Set a modest daily quotient*
9. *Quit while you're ahead; do not exhaust yourself*
10. *Plan and execute a reward for work well done*

Telltale Temperament

THE MORNING LIGHT in Taos Valley is even and clear. Chicory stands sentinel by the roadside. Red-winged blackbirds dart among the willows. Ravens and magpies sail overhead, crisscrossing the sky with their cries. After a rainfall, the valley is washed clean. Everything looks new. You would think, from the sheer racket of birdsong, that we were celebrating the first morning of all. When Mabel Dodge, an heiress and socialite, married a Pueblo Indian, Tony Luhan, she began inviting her far-flung cosmopolitan friends to come and visit her new homestead. D. H. Lawrence came—and is buried north of Taos. Georgia O'Keeffe came, paintbrush in hand. Artists of all stripes followed, drawn to the valley by its great beauty and the quality of the light.

As surely as the Tewa Indians, whose pueblo is the oldest inhabited dwelling in North America, artists, too, constitute a tribe. Just as a trace of Native American blood may show in the shape of a cheekbone, there are telltale signs that identify the artist. All beings are creative; that is our nature. But artists are committed to their creativity, dedicated to serving it. This vocation brings a certain vividness to the personality. In Taos, where many artists live and hold a variety of day jobs, it is not uncommon to discover that a waitress or clerk is a painter of estimable power. Because so many artists gravitate to Taos, and so few support themselves solely by their art, it is dangerous here to assume that a waiter is "merely" a waiter, or a clerk a clerk.

Shambhu Vaughan, a waiter at Lambert's, paints still lifes and plays blues guitar. A fine waiter, he is distinguished by his precise service and upright bearing. His dignity is instantly apparent. "Like being waited on by a king," visitors have remarked. There is, in most artists, a lively attention and quicksilver humor. These qualities are found in abundance in Taos. So is an attitude of "We're all in this together," "this" being the art of making art. Not all artists are quick-witted and emotionally nimble. But many are. A smile lurks at the corner of a mouth, the eyes wrinkle with laughter. Sometimes, a renegade red slip peeps roguishly out from a waitress uniform. Halloween, with its emphasis on costumes and creativity, is the town's favorite holiday. Artists have a capacity to look at things differently, to see below the surface to the quick of things. And that word "quick" is no accident either. Alive to the moment, artists are quick and responsive. They have to be to make art. Art is a matter of receptivity. We become open both to the muse and the moment. Is it any wonder artists find so many things amusing?

The morning light in Taos Valley is so clean, it emphasizes particularity. Every blade of grass, every Russian olive tree gleaming silver, every grosbeak, every tiny finch demands "Notice me! See what a miracle I am!" As artists, we are all miraculous, ever-changing, always making something new from what has come before. Our eye might light anywhere. That gray satin river rock, does it suggest a sculpture? That gently lofted tuft of cottonwood, is it time for a note of whimsy? That artist lives in a state of readiness, open to the world around him, well aware, as M.C. Richards writes, that "inspiration enters through the window of irrelevance." With the bright, clear light of a Taos morning, is it any wonder the windows are flung open?

Try this: All artists need encouragement. We need the sense of support that comes from tribal elders. And yet, too often we are isolated from other artists. And so we must strategize to reinforce our artist identity. Scrutinize the following list, select one action you can take, and take it.

1. *Buy and read an autobiography of an artist working in your chosen arena*
2. *Rent and view a video about another artist working in your chosen arena*
3. *Subscribe to a magazine related to your chosen arena*
4. *Attend a conference in your area of interest (for example, Romance Writers of America)*
5. *Attend a workshop in support of your art*

Any action taken in support of our artist is an action that strengthens us. Sometimes the act of supporting another artist by attending a gallery opening or play reading is an act that reinforces our identity as well as theirs. It is important as an artist to nurture a sense of belonging and shared burdens. A simple coffee date with another artist can often break our sense of isolation. Schedule one such date.

Survival Lessons

WHEN THE STUDENT IS WILLING, the teacher appears, spiritual sages tell us. Another way to put it is that when we are willing to be taught, we become teachable. We always move ahead in our art when we open our heart to willingness. In order to do something well, we must first be willing to do it badly. We must have the humility to be once again a beginner, to admit what we don't know and admit that we wish to know more. It could be argued that it takes an artist to teach an artist. It is certainly true that the voice of hard-won experience is always educational. But artists can learn from nonartists as well. A master chef, choreographing a perfectly served meal, might teach us the value of presentation. A kindergarten teacher might teach us the worth of patience. From a master baker we might learn tenderness and precision. Teachers are everywhere when we are open to them.

But we cannot learn everything at once. We must first learn progress, not perfection. Too often, we measure our early creative attempts against the masterworks of accomplished artists. Falling short, we become discouraged. We have not witnessed their learning curve. We have seen the *Godfather* trilogy, not Coppola's beginning films. In our imagination, the early works of accomplished artists must be marked by genius. It isn't always so. Art is a combination of talent and character, and many times the artists who win do so because of their stubbornness. They refuse to take no for an answer. Others among us, fearful of the big arena, take no for an answer much too readily. The slightest discouragement sends us scurrying into creative U-turns, ducking for cover, lest any more harsh words be said or printed. Part of what the veteran artist teaches is how to survive a career. It takes courage to make another film after a round of bad reviews. It takes courage to write a novel or paint. One of the benefits of aligning ourselves with veteran artists is that they have such courage, and have mustered it decade in and decade out.

Recently, I attended a chamber music concert, a very fine one to my ear. The first half of the program featured a quintet, and after intermission I noticed I was sitting very close to a musician who had finished his work for the night. This was a famous musician, a man known and sought after for his superior sound. Yet as I watched from the corner of my eye, I saw him bury his head in his hands, despairing. Less than a week later, at a second concert, I saw the same musician stride forcefully to center stage and take his place. This was a lesson for me in courage, a lesson in backing down the censor who tells us that every performance must be perfect.

Another friend of mine recently returned from a ten-city book tour where the crowds ranged from small to nearly nonexistent. This was a best-selling author, but not recently. No longer flavor of the month, my writer friend ruefully recollected the empty venues and the toll they took on her professional pride. "Sometimes I would get to a bookstore and discover there was another author scheduled simultaneously," she recounted. From these stories, I took a lesson in professionalism, in the pride of doing a good job no matter how small the audience. Like Jack the show horse, my friend had standards, a level of performance to measure up to. A career will have ups and a career will have downs. What the veteran teaches us is how to survive them. Over any considerable period of time, a creative career resembles an athletic career, and just as our sports heroes win our admiration by playing through despite pain and injury, so, too, do our veteran artists.

SURVIVAL LESSONS

Try this: Many of us have arenas where we know we need additional skills but we are afraid to enter. The first step in getting help is admitting that we need it. Take pen in hand and finish the following phrase as rapidly as possible:

1. *If I let myself admit it, I could learn more about* _____.
2. *If I let myself admit it, I could learn more about* _____.
3. *If I let myself admit it, I could learn more about* _____.
4. *If I let myself admit it, I could learn more about* _____.
5. *If I let myself admit it, I could learn more about* _____.

6. *If I let myself admit it, I could learn more*
   about _____.
7. *If I let myself admit it, I could learn more*
   about _____.
8. *If I let myself admit it, I could learn more*
   about _____.
9. *If I let myself admit it, I could learn more*
   about _____.
10. *If I let myself admit it, I could learn more*
    about _____.

Choose one activity from this list, and allow
yourself to be teachable.

Creative Equality

THE ENTIRE SKY is a canyon of clouds. The mountains to the north are bolstered by thunderheads. The mountains to the south lie under puffy cumulus. To the west, over the mesa, stalks walking rain, long-legged dark gray clouds that move like giants across the sage. Directly overhead is a shock of bright blue weather, a small patch of azure rapidly losing ground to the billowing clouds. The weather in Taos Valley changes hourly, and sometimes, it seems, minute by minute. There is an alarming propensity toward rainbows; I've seen as many as three arcing horizon to horizon. Several times, my house has been at the end of the rainbow, and I have needed to ask myself, "What is the pot of gold here?" The answer, always, is creativity.

The other day I spoke to a lady writer. She asked what I was doing these days, and I told her, more and more music, and long afternoons of prose. "Congratulations," she told me. "Music is higher than writing. You're moving up an octave." "Thank you," I managed to say, wondering if I agreed. To me, the entire notion of "higher than" and "better than" smacks of an elitism that closes more doors than it opens. The distinction between the fine arts, for example, and the decorative arts is often lost on me. What makes a Jackson Pollock more valuable or artistic than a hand-blown vase? Both are beautiful, each in its way. Both are unique— why must there be a pecking order? Why must one art form outrank another? Why must one artist be called an artist and another an artisan?

Perhaps I take my ideas of art more from the natural world. Is a Russian olive, shining silver in the sun, less beautiful than an orchid? Is an orchid, in its snowy perfection, more beautiful than a gray satin river rock? The Great Creator seems to have found beauty in diversity. We have rain forests and the vast sweep of the Sahara. We have maple trees and cacti. We have the rock-ribbed, craggy terrain of Sicily and the gentle, mossy green hills of the Emerald Isle. As artists, we do best to be discerning but not snobbish. There is beauty to be found in a child's drawing and beauty to be found in a Dürer print. Calder can appeal to us, and so can Degas. We may admire both Stieglitz and O'Keeffe. True, we will have our favorites among them, but that doesn't mean we need to damn the others as lesser art. We can have preferences without having prejudice.

America invented the assembly line, and it is to this invention that we owe what I call our "lug-bolt mentality." In America we are urged to be good at one thing and stick to it, to create a recognizable brand name, as it were. In America we are warned not to be dilettantes, as if straying from one enthusiasm to another is a capital crime. Europeans are far more forgiving of diversity. An English writer can, and often does, write in many forms without sullying his reputation. Not so in America. My lady writer friend explains it to me: "Poetry is higher than prose, but music is higher than poetry." Her distinctions leave me unsettled. What of the beauty of musical prose? I wonder. To my eye, some of the greatest artists have ignored distinctions.

David Hockney is a fine painter, a master of the line drawing, and a maestro of the operatic set. He is also a very stubborn man who has been critically punished for moving from arena to arena. Picasso, to point out another familiar example, moved from form to form throughout his career. He had his blue period, his rose period, and that long period where he made whimsical junkyard sculptures from found objects—among many other phases. We must be free to follow our own readings rather than follow trends. It is for this reason that the connoisseur's distinctions among the arts do not always serve us. We cannot afford to take too seriously the idea that children's books or teen literature are lesser than the Great American Novel. We cannot peg performance art below playwriting, or the Broadway musical below Beethoven. We must be free to follow our muse, and often that means what amuses us. We cannot subscribe to the Academy Awards convention that comedy is a lower art form than tragedy and less deserving of Oscar's nod. Carl Jung has remarked that creativity is the imagination at play with things it loves. Play is a child's favorite activity. Young children do not engage in snobbery. As Oscar Hammerstein observed, "You've got to be carefully taught."

A photographer training his lens on Taos Valley today would be hard-pressed to choose a direction. Dramatic cloud forms unfold in all directions. They are all beautiful.

CREATIVE
EQUALITY

Try this: Artists are curious beings. Most of us
have interests and enthusiasms that fall outside
our declared arena. These interests and enthusiasms feed us. They are good for our soul and
good for our art. Take pen in hand. Number
from 1 to 10. Complete the following phrase as
rapidly as possible:

    1. *I am secretly interested in*

    _____.

    2. *I am secretly interested in*

    _____.

    3. *I am secretly interested in*

    _____.

    4. *I am secretly interested in*

    _____.

    5. *I am secretly interested in*

    _____.

6. *I am secretly interested in*
   _____.

7. *I am secretly interested in*
   _____.

8. *I am secretly interested in*
   _____.

9. *I am secretly interested in*
   _____.

10. *I am secretly interested in*
    _____.

Very often our list of secret enthusiasms
yields us a topic on which we can happily make
art. Review your list. Is there such a topic?

Staying in Touch

TOWERING THUNDERHEADS loom over Taos Mountain. They are snowy white and showy. The rest of the sky is an azure bowl, vast, hot, and empty. Much of New Mexico is empty. Highways crisscross vast sage fields; mesas and buttes rise above those. It is often difficult to raise a signal for a cell phone. They work only near communities, and sometimes they don't work at all. Many an old adobe house features the addition of a modern satellite dish, a great glistening ear that scoops information from space. It is possible here to be very connected to the earth and its cycles and very disconnected from the flow of human events. The war in the Middle East, global warming—these things seem distant here. It takes an effort, a special trip to town, to buy the Sunday *New York Times* in order to stay in touch with modern life. That, or the purchase of a satellite dish.

Many times, when we are involved in a creative project, we put a psychological distance between ourselves and ordinary modern life. Our attention is on the novel, the film, the series we are painting. These things loom as large and eminent as Taos Mountain, dwarfing everything else by comparison.

Edward, a writer, puts it this way: "When I am absorbed by my writing, it is in Technicolor, and the rest of the world is black and white." Judith, a painter, agrees. "When I'm deep in my painting, the world falls away. My world becomes the painting—that is all that matters to me. Minutes, hours, and sometimes days slip past. On some projects, months and years." We live within the weather of our work, and that weather may differ from that of the world around us.

In a sense, left to our own devices, artists can be like cave dwellers, disappearing into the murk of the subconscious, to fish there for images and meaning. An artist's life can all too readily lose its grounding in the outer world. If we allow this to happen, we emerge from our work, blinking and dazzled by the blinding glare of collective reality. Because our inner worlds are so compelling, artists must make a special effort to remain connected to the outer world. While we cannot be as connected as many other people—living with a constantly ringing phone, for example, or the constant presence of CNN—we *can* stay connected by doing modern life in small doses. Many artists manage their media diet— one newsmagazine per week, fifteen minutes daily of the news at eleven, a once-a-week immersion in the Sunday *Times.* We need the flow of outer life to both balance and sustain the flow of inner life. Our art is simultaneously removed from, and reflective of, society as a whole.

For many artists, e-mail is a mixed blessing. Easily addictive yet highly connective, it works best for us as an addition to our art rather than as a substitute for it. The danger of e-mail is that in our hunger for connection, we pour out our creative energies into a barrage of letters instead of onto the easel or page. The advantage of e-mail and use of the Internet as a whole is that it cuts through feelings of intense isolation, connecting us to like-minded souls even when we are geographically far-flung. Make no mistake: Art can take us to distant places, to caves buried deep within the psyche, or to the wide expanses of distant space. If a reader loses all sense of time when entering the world, say, of J. K. Rowling, how much more hypnotic must that world be for its maker? Artists require careful grounding. We must remember to eat, to sleep, to reach out and touch someone, if only electronically. It is all too easy for an artist to abandon life as the rest of the world knows it, to live on a different planet while right in our midst. Art is powerful. The making of art is so powerful that folklore abounds with tales of the eccentricities of artists: the way they button their shirts backward, forget to tie their shoes, leave their hair unbrushed, and the like. Artists need wives and husbands who truly husband. Failing such connections that remind us to eat, to sleep, to talk, we must carefully manage such things for ourselves. It is best, therefore, not to binge on our creativity but to keep it carefully embedded in the daily flow of life. A novelist may do well to keep bankers' hours. Artists require structure and may often need to build structure in order to have it. A modest daily quotient of art quickly builds upon itself. This is where that familiar 12-step slogan "Easy does it" comes into play. If we work regularly, and in smaller increments, we will work more readily. If we binge on our work, we will overfish our creative trout pond, and then it will take longer for us to work as we struggle to find the images that we seek.

It is a matter of balance. An artist must be immersed in life without being submerged in it. An artist must have enough solitude and enough connection. It takes practice, and it takes the conscious building of daily ritual. There are friends with whom we can maintain a light, continuous contact. There are television and other news sources that can keep us grounded in national and international affairs. *The Christian Science Monitor,* for example, is a highly objective and succinct news source, and it is available over the Internet.

Just as the satellite dish scoops from space an astounding plethora of channels, so, too, does modern life offer us an astonishing array of diversions. Overindulged in, the media world becomes toxic to our art, flooding it with a surplus of information and detail. Underencountered, the world of affairs whirls past us as a dizzying confusion. We can feel too helpless and too underinformed to take our place as citizens. Each of us must determine for ourselves, and in the light of our own creative productivity, the amount and the type of outside information we can allow to enter our sphere. It is a matter of experimentation. Jean, a painter, allows herself talk radio and Books on Tape when she is in the preparatory phases of her art. During the actual periods of painting, she switches the dial of her radio to a classical station, lending credence to the notion that there actually is a "Mozart effect," and that certain forms of music can heighten rather than deaden our creativity. Paul, a concert pianist, finds that he must curtail his immersion in political affairs during those periods when he must practice most rigorously. "I can't afford to get too worried," he explains. "I have to worry about my concert first and foremost. The world needs to get along without me for a few days." Edmund, a novelist, has a theory that most of us attune ourselves to political affairs like the fearful flier who believes he keeps the plane aloft by his firm grip on his armrests. "I have had to learn," says Edmund, "to pull my consciousness somewhat back from world events. My worried concentration on international politics doesn't really affect the war in the Middle East or the possibility of another terrorist attack. While I want to be informed, I do not want or need to be overinformed. I've had to learn this."

The vast New Mexico sky arches blue and serene over human affairs. At 9,200 feet, in Taos Ski Valley, a cell phone picks up a faint but definite signal. How we use it is up to us.

Try this: As creative beings, we must learn to tune in to, not tune out from, our environment. When we take the time and care to husband the life we've been given, we are able to gently nudge that life a little closer to the life we desire. Here is another Filling in the Form exercise. Take pen in hand and number from 1 to 5. List five tiny changes you can make to improve the serenity and clarity of your environment. For example:

1. *Make my bed every day*
2. *Throw out extra papers*
3. *Get a letter basket*
4. *Sort through my closet and throw away "oldies but moldies"*
5. *Use a good enamel to repaint the chipped kitchen chair*

While none of these actions focuses directly on our creative projects, all of these actions help us to focus. Select one tiny change and execute it.

Sudden Inspiration

WHEN IT RAINS in the high mountains of New Mexico, there is always the factual danger of a lightning strike. Postcards of New Mexico like to feature such strikes. The cards are dramatic, but not nearly so dramatic as the event. Sometimes, the lightning stalks across the ridges like great golden legs walking closer. Sometimes it strikes out on the mesa, illuminating a lunar field of sage. Like the rattlesnake, the lightning strike is an ever-present danger. As with the snake, the odds of getting struck are slight—but real.

Sometimes in our creative life, inspiration does come to us in a blinding flash. The bolt of illumination reveals an entire piece of work in stark relief. Information floods in on our startled senses. There is an uncanny certainty and precision about what we see. Like a lightning strike, it is definitive: This is how it is, how it must be. Now do it. The doing of it can be very daunting. Speaking for myself, I have been four times struck by sudden bolts of music. Although I am told I do it backward, the music for my musicals comes to me first—in great, sudden swaths. I race to capture the melodies as they seem to tumble into my head, complete with lyrics. I feel I will never keep up. Sometimes the music comes so suddenly and so fast that I must sing it into tape recorders for later transcription. Always, such sudden storms of music leave me shaken, electrified. I am so "lit up" by the bolt of inspiration that my creative surge can resemble mania and cause people to wonder whether I am having a breakdown—or a breakthrough. It is, of course, the music itself that holds the answer, and I have found that the music received in such a sudden and cataclysmic way does indeed have surpassing beauty to recommend it.

Far more often, creativity is a less dramatic, more daily affair. Inspiration comes not in bolts, but in inklings. Usually I hear music a few notes at a time, as though I am being led gently down a garden path, following a trail of notes. It is nice when creativity is so friendly and inviting. And most of the time, for most of us, it is. Our folklore, of course, is filled with dramatic stories. We hear of first drafts scribbled down in days. We hear of music that visited like a sudden fever. These stories are just stories, and we like them for their drama, but they are not the norm. Just as on many days the rainfall comes in gentle sheets with lightning far away, and on many days you can walk the sage fields without once spotting a snake.

My first musical, *Avalon,* struck me like lightning. I had never "heard" music before, and suddenly it was flooding through me in great surges. By the time *Magellan* came to me, I knew enough to tell my worried husband, "It's just music. Don't worry." When *The Medium at Large* landed as a rapid and sudden set of songs, I knew enough to eat and sleep—as well as write them down. When lightning strikes creatively, it is very important that we keep our grounding, that we remember that as important as the work seems, we, too, are important and must be cared for. It is romantic nonsense to sacrifice ourselves on the altar of art. A lack of sleep, a lack of food, a lack of companionship—all of these heighten our already heightened state. A lack of sleep induces psychosis, and we do not need that, we need art. Friends and families can be warned that

we are in the creative rapids and reassured that as the name suggests, such rapids will pass rapidly. Just as a well-built house has
lightning rods for grounding, we as artists can choose among our
friends those who are able to encompass the surges of creativity
that sometimes come to us. "I'm in the rapids," we might say. "Are
you sleeping? Remember to eat," our friend might reply. With
practice, we *can* sleep, and we do eat. With faith, we remember
that the bolt of inspiration was strong enough to leave a lasting
imprint, and that we will be strong enough to carry our vision
fully to fruition. It needn't all be done at once. Even a rainstorm
can continue to pelt down after the lightning has passed.

SUDDEN
INSPIRATION

Try this: When sudden inspiration hits us, we may be shaken and doubt our own ability to follow through. It is at times like this that we need the encouragement of an elder mentor. It is possible, and useful, to access a wise mentor. To do this, set aside one half hour. Take pen in hand and write yourself a letter of encouragement, using the persona of an older and wiser and admired artist. You may wish to mail yourself this letter.

Local Color

ON THE HIGH MOUNTAIN RIDGES, dark conifers stand stark sentinels against the sky. Taos is in the high desert, and within its reaches it holds five vegetation zones, ranging from desert to alpine. Lilacs flourish here, but so do cacti. Tulips, peonies, and jonquils thrive, but so do chamiso and sage. Just as the vegetation zones vary wildly as you gain altitude, climbing from the valley lowlands to Wheeler Peak, so, too, do the townspeople present a colorful and varied mix. Of course they do—there is a very high proportion of declared artists among them, and many others practice creativity in some form. Your short-order chef at the hot dog stand may be a novelist, your housepainter may be an acclaimed portraitist. There's no stigma in Taos to having a day job—sometimes several. The economy is poor, the beauty of the landscape rich, and people make their peace between the two.

Novelist John Nichols lives in a tumbledown adobe sheltered by a small stand of aspen. Sunflowers tower along his garden fence. Nichols makes his way around town by bicycle and battered truck. An award-winning writer, he is as whimsical and particular as any of his creations.

Sculptor Kevin Cannon lives in an ancient adobe with tiny odd-size rooms. His studio windows are hung with muslin to prevent him from being distracted by the dazzling views. Cannon works in leather. His sculptures are collected internationally. Like

Nichols, he favors a bicycle for his trips to the post office. For his drives to Santa Fe, he uses a well-kept vintage Volvo in a red the color of sangria.

Novelist Natalie Goldberg lives in an exotic underground house called an "earth ship." Hers is located amid sage fields out on the mesa, and she must use a fine wire mesh on her chimney lest she be visited in her home by curious rabbits and snakes. Goldberg prefers walking to any other mode of transportation. She has a car, a used Subaru, for the long drive into town, but once there, she parks and travels by foot.

As these few examples show, Taos is a bouquet of varied artists. A cocktail party in Taos, or an art show opening, displays a rogue's gallery of colorful archetypes. Sometimes I think the town is like a scientific experiment, a hothouse environment in which artists grow and flourish. According to our mythology, artists are distant creatures, unable to mix well socially. This is not my experience. In Taos, artists are Joe Citizen, turning out to clean the ditches on Ditch Day. Many artists are themselves gardeners. Goldberg's house features a solar underground garden illuminated by wildflowers. Painter Peter Ziminsky paints entire landscapes in his day job as a landscape architect.

Taos is a chockablock community. Zoning laws are nearly nonexistent—a half-million-dollar adobe villa may adjoin a double-wide house trailer. A log cabin may abut a house made of recycled Coke bottles and tires. Malcolm Brown's house surges like a ship's prow above the valley meadows. The Double D Ranch looks like a frontier town from the outside but features a sushi restaurant and artificially cantilevered waterfalls for showers. Since the days of the original painters who settled Taos, creativity has been expressed in myriad ways. Mabel Dodge Luhan tinted the wooden vigas of her ceiling in rainbow hues. Leon Gaspard, a Russian, managed to give his adobe villa a Russian flavor. Sometimes Taosenos joke about their diversity. Violin maker Charles Erwin lives on a ranch the size of a taco chip. "Medicine Dog Ranch," his homestead is dubbed, named for Ervin's distinctive pack of guard dogs.

In Taos, a Hollywood set designer might do the scenery for a high school play. An Oscar-nominated screenwriter might participate at an open mic poetry event. Halloween is the community's favorite holiday, and costumes appear everywhere, from Wal-Mart to the Chevron station. Fathers dress as vampires, mothers go to town as Elvira, Mistress of the Dark. There is a festivity inherent in all this creativity, a gentle sense of permission pervading the town. It is as though the community logo is "anything goes—and let's see what you come up with." Like the five vegetation zones blooming side by side, Taos is a demonstration that creativity creates a human garden.

LOCAL COLOR

Try this: Each of us is colorful and unique. Each of us displays our creativity by the choices we make. Some choices are more relevant than others. They seem to sum up, or embody, our value system. Take pen in hand and number from 1 to 5. List five choices that you are proud of, choices that seem quintessentially you. For example:

1. *I danced center on kickline in college*
2. *I helped my sibling financially during a divorce*
3. *I wrote and published a short-story collection*
4. *I stood up to the classroom bully*
5. *I got sober and made sobriety my priority*

Set aside another half hour's time. Pen in hand, explore just what it was about each choice that seemed so important and particular to you. Is there a choice you can now make that would fill you with pride and satisfaction?

The Longer View

THE FOREST FIRES that stormed across the Southwest, burning large stretches through Arizona, Colorado, and New Mexico, have been contained. Strong rains have come and rinsed clear the smoke- and soot-laden atmosphere. Now you can see distance. In Taos Valley, mountain range upon mountain range unfolds to the east, north, and south. To the west, a vast mesa studded with sage stretches to a far horizon, also marked by a range of mountains.

The ability to see distance is critical to a creative career. We must always bear in mind that each day's work is part of a larger body of work, and that body of work is the work of a lifetime. Unless we are able to take and maintain this long view, we are apt to be derailed by any rejection. One discouraging letter, and the novel goes into a drawer, never to be submitted again. One surly gallery owner, and our canvases get retired to the garage, never again to make the rounds. "What's the use," we may say, and stop writing or painting. Artists are easily bruised. This is why we retain agents and dealers to handle our rejection for us. I once shared a literary agent with William Kennedy, the author of *Iron-weed,* winner of the Pulitzer Prize. Our agent told me he submitted *Ironweed* fifty times before he had a bite. Was Kennedy any less a writer while those rejections were unfurling? No. Being published, being in a gallery, or being currently employed as an actor does not make us a "real" artist. Doing the work does—showing up at the page, the easel, the rehearsal hall, and putting in our hours.

Seen in the long view, one stinging rejection does not unmake a career. But the long view can be hard to hold on to by ourselves. I have published several books, well reviewed and well received, that initially met with discouragement. "No one would read *The Artist's Way*," I was told, a prediction that was off by about two million readers. "This book would ruin your career," I was told about *Popcorn*, a well-thought-of collection of short stories. My crime novel, *The Dark Room*, also met with dire predictions, only to sell well and receive good reviews. In each of these circumstances, I relied on my Believing Mirrors to cheer me through the acute depression that my naysayers induced. We need stratagems to survive rejection. Like Hal Prince, director John Newland always scheduled a meeting on a new project for the morning after opening night. A veteran writer of my acquaintance has made a rule to make one new submission for every rejection received. A well-thumbed *Writer's Market* is a trusted ally.

Just as the smoke from the forest fires erased the mountain ranges, so, too, can we go blind and lose our perspective when faced with a harsh rejection. Even the most seasoned writer or filmmaker has difficulty shrugging off a bad review. Many novelists and directors do not read their reviews until long after the fact, if then. Actress Julianna McCarthy states the problem this way: "If you're going to believe your good reviews, then you have to believe your bad reviews." She believes a good review can do as much damage to a performer as a tough one. "You start trying to imitate yourself, and the next thing you know, the performance is dead." It helps to think of our life's work in terms of portrait painting: Our work is the subject, front and center, but our lives are the background that gives us context. That background is the longer view.

Try this: Take pen in hand. Number from 1 to 10 and finish the following phrase as rapidly as possible:

1. *If I took the long view, I'd*

   _____.

2. *If I took the long view, I'd*

   _____.

3. *If I took the long view, I'd*

   _____.

4. *If I took the long view, I'd*

   _____.

5. *If I took the long view, I'd*

   _____.

6. *If I took the long view, I'd*

   _____.

7. *If I took the long view, I'd*

   _____.

8. *If I took the long view, I'd*

   _____.

9. *If I took the long view, I'd*

   _____.

10. *If I took the long view, I'd*

   _____.

Landmarks

AT EMBUDO, NEW MEXICO, the Rio Grande and Embudo River intersect at a cross. On a mountaintop, high above this juncture, stands a white, snowy cross. Eagles nest in the cliffs below the cross. They soar out over the rivers, hunting for food to return to their young. The great cross oversees their activities. Like the floral-wreathed crosses that stud the roadside, it is a reminder, a memento mori. We are all mortal, the cross declares, and one day we will each of us pass from this sphere.

Beneath the foot of the mountain where the cross stands sentinel, the Rio Grande curves on its glistening green way. If the cross is a reminder of our deaths, the river, with its living waters teeming with trout, is a reminder of life. It has been said that we make art in order to be immortal, in order to leave something behind. Perhaps we do. But we also make art to fulfill our days among the living. Just as the river quietly flows, we proceed at our work. On rising, I write Morning Pages. They help prioritize my day and show me when and how I can find the time to make my art. A brief Walk sandwiched in between phone calls and appointments tells me *how* to make my art. Tangled plotlines and stifled songs untangle as I walk. It is in dailiness that art is born.

Writer Sophy Burnham estimates it takes her ten years to make a book. She sometimes works on more than one at a time, alternating projects in her daily sessions at her desk in the study of the brick town house where she has lived now for thirty years. "I write a draft, then I let it breathe for a while, and when I come back to it, I have a new perspective," she explains. In her time, Burnham has written plays, novels, and three best-selling works of nonfiction. She is a writer of the first water, and above all else, a worker. She works daily.

Sculptor Kevin Cannon is another daily worker, rising early in his old adobe home, making himself a small breakfast and retiring for a long day's work in his studio, where he makes very beautiful sculptures from leather. After each piece is finished, he makes a meticulous charcoal drawing of it, often as beautiful as the sculpture itself. Collected internationally, Cannon prefers to work in the anonymity he finds in Taos. There, the beauty of the landscape and sky feed his artist's eye and he is undistracted by the din of the large city as he works. A jazz guitarist by avocation, Cannon can be found playing small local gigs on winter evenings. Although a very fine guitarist, he still holds himself an amateur, reminding one of the word's root in the Latin verb *amare*, "to love."

It is our love of art, of the process of making art, that draws us to our daily work. Artists are committed to the making of art, although we often toil for years without a sentinel landmark, like that cross, to remind us of our path. My first musical, *Avalon,* was seven years in the making. *Magellan,* an opera, unfurled in six. In the final stages of each project, demos were made. It was exciting and unnerving to suddenly have physical, auditory proof of the long process my musical collaborator and I had undergone—suddenly we had a landmark for our creative travels.

Recently, I gave a dinner party that another writer attended. "Would you like to see where I work?" I asked him. "Oh, I would," he answered. And so I led him up the stairs to the small crimson room where an old wooden desk held my IBM Selectric and a sheaf of papers. "I love Selectrics," the writer enthused. "I work on a computer now, but I've been thinking of getting myself a Selectric again. There's something about them that just invites writing, isn't there?" "Yes," I said. "I think it's their sound. They're companionable, like a horse trotting along. A typewriter keeps you company while you write." The writer nodded agreement. Neither of us needed reminding that in our daily march, we went to our writing alone, like a monk to his cell.

As artists, we want and need encouragement. This may be why some artists are superstitious, writing with a special pen in a certain notebook, at a certain spot. Perhaps we could use a sentinel cross to mark the mountain of our work.

LANDMARKS

Try this: Go to the five-and-dime. Select a large photo album, the kind that allows you to place an entire sheet of paper behind the cellophane shield. This is your landmark book. Use it as a scrapbook for your own creative projects. Every project generates a trail marking its progress. Yours may include letters, ticket stubs, recorded compliments, reading dates, gallery invitations, and photos of special occasions. Allow this creativity scrapbook to document the landmarks of your progress.

Build It, and
They Will Come

QUESTA, NEW MEXICO, is located in the mountain valley at
7,500 feet. High peaks soar at its perimeter. Coming into the town,
there are two landmarks: the White Dove Laundromat, and a log
cabin labeled Paloma Blanca Coffee House. Run by a mother with
her two daughters, the Paloma Blanca features homemade pastries
and fine coffee. I am not the only Taoseno who drives twenty-odd
miles for a cup of their brew. Taos itself is well stocked with coffee
shops: the North and South Bean, the World Cup, Café Tazza, and
Inspirations, to name just a handful. Still, none of them holds a candle to the coffee at Paloma Blanca. It is worth the drive.

Often, as artists, we doubt that mere excellence is enough to
attract our good. We buy into negative and self-defeating notions
like "I have to live in New York; I have to know the right people;
I have to have an agent; I have to do almost anything that strikes
me as impossible in my current circumstances." A few years back,
there was a fine movie called *Field of Dreams*. In it, the hero was
directed to build a major-league ball field amid his corn crop.
It would be a great tourist attraction, he was told. "Here?" he
protested. "In the middle of nowhere, in the middle of a corn-
field?" His guidance reassured him: "Build it, and they will come."

"Build it, and they will come" is profound creative advice. It puts
the emphasis on process rather than on product. It emphasizes the

fact that artists lead rather than follow the market. Too often, artists get sidetracked trying to market their work before it is finished. They write book proposals instead of books, screen treatments instead of screenplays. Meanwhile, precious weeks, months, and years tick by.

Often, when I advise a writer to write a whole book rather than a proposal, I am greeted with "But, Julia! I don't want to do all that work for nothing." But we never do all that work for nothing. When we write, we become better writers. When we paint, we become better painters. Dancing improves our dancing, acting our acting. Art lies in doing, and an artist who creates freely has a certain allure. A wild horse is more mysterious and attractive than its domesticated brother.

When we look for a guarantee of success, we are asking to make risk-free art, and art, by definition, is risky. We are always seeking to express that which has not been expressed. One of the many difficulties with book treatments is that the finished book lacks the same zest as the treatment. Of course it does. We are saying twice what we have said once in the best way that came to us. Editors complain that sometimes a finished book bears no resemblance to the proposal they bought. This is because the writer was unable to replicate his proposal. Instead, like all real artists, he followed his muse into new and trickier territory.

Art for art's sake, like the wild mustang, has the power of attraction going for it. There is something irresistible about what cannot be owned. When we make art from the inside out rather than from the outside in, when we commit to letting the market find us rather than prematurely seeking the market, our art has a chance to incubate and become more powerful without the diluting effect of outside influences. An artist is a sensitive and volatile creature. Easily discouraged, an artist can give up on a promising new direction if cold water is showered upon his dream. For this reason, all art-making deserves our protection. We call artistic creations brain*children* for a reason. When thoughts of the market are introduced too early, it is like bludgeoning a kindergarten pupil about getting grades good enough to go to college. This is not to say that we do not consider the market eventually, that we do not take timely steps to promote our art, but the key word there is *timely*, and as a rule of thumb it is better that we seek the market too late than too early.

Art is a time-consuming process, and in our youth-oriented culture of instant gratification, this is not a popular thing to say. I have had plays take fifteen years to get into production, novels that have taken a decade to make it into print. Sometimes the market needed to mature to match the material. Other times, the material needed to mature to match the market. Meanwhile, in the time elapsed, I wrote new things—with the result that, like many artists, I am wealthy with my own material. Novelist John Nichols worked a dozen years on his novel *The Voice of the Butterfly*. There was no contract guaranteeing that the book would ever be bought, and yet Nichols worked night after night, year in and year out, draft to draft, to assure its successful completion. The same can be said of all artists. It is the practice of our art form, and not the marketable product we produce, that warrants us the name artist.

BUILD IT, AND
THEY WILL COME

Try this: Take pen in hand. Number from 1 to
10. Finish this phrase as rapidly as possible:

1. *If I believed in a benevolent universe, I'd try*
   _____.

2. *If I believed in a benevolent universe, I'd try*
   _____.

3. *If I believed in a benevolent universe, I'd try*
   _____.

4. *If I believed in a benevolent universe, I'd try*
   _____.

5. *If I believed in a benevolent universe, I'd try*
   _____.

6. *If I believed in a benevolent universe, I'd try*
   _____.

7. *If I believed in a benevolent universe, I'd try*

   _____.

8. *If I believed in a benevolent universe, I'd try*

   _____.

9. *If I believed in a benevolent universe, I'd try*

   _____.

10. *If I believed in a benevolent universe, I'd try*

   _____.

Some of what you've been procrastinating about may surprise you. Select one action from your list and begin it.

Achieving Altitude

LA VETA PASS, altitude 9,413 feet, drops down from Colorado into the San Luis Valley, which in turn opens to the hunting grounds near the Costilla River and the entry to New Mexico. Although state lines look arbitrary and neutral when viewed on a map, when experienced driving they often mark perceptible shifts in territory and terrain. Both Colorado and New Mexico are mountainous, but the Colorado peaks are the jagged, masculine Rockies, while New Mexico's contours are more rounded and feminine. "The Land of Enchantment," New Mexico is called, and it lives up to its name. Wreathed in clouds like the Dance of the Seven Veils, New Mexico lacks Colorado's macho bravado and attains instead an aura of mystery. It is no accident that so many artists make their homes in New Mexico. The constantly changing landscape is a good match for the creative psyche. In New Mexico, nothing looks today exactly as it did yesterday. The same shifting weather accompanies a long creative project.

Seasoned artists know the wisdom of ignoring each day's opinion of the unfolding work. A dark mood can color critical perceptions. Today's junk may be tomorrow's gold, as a sunnier mood makes the work look worthwhile. Because our emotional weather is so capricious, we must learn to let it pass through without acting destructively on its invitations. Brahms destroyed twelve string quartets. He left only three. Beethoven refused to dignify many fine early works with an opus number. His legacy? A welter of conflicting manuscripts, corrected and corrected again. Bach, on the other hand, had to write a weekly cantata for the church where he worked. Too pressed by deadlines to have time for negative critical considerations, he routinely produced masterworks.

"Julia," I am often asked, "what if you are unblocking a lot of bad artists?" I think this is the wrong question. In my twenty-plus years of teaching, I have far more often seen fine artists hang back, hamstrung by low self-worth. A quick glance at the market is enough to convince almost anyone that it is often artistic nerve, not merit, that moves someone center stage. That being the case, we need to temper our self-destructive tendency to overcensor.

Andrew has written several novels, but none of them measured up to his inner standards for "good work." He loved to write and was afraid to publish. His novels enjoyed one another's company in a large bottom desk drawer. Andrew's publishing history might have continued this way, except for the timely intervention of a new friend. "Come on, Andrew," she wheedled, "let me read at least one." Andrew relented, and gave her an early novel to read. "But this is *good!*" his friend exclaimed, returning the manuscript. "I don't see why you don't publish!" Andrew told her a sad story about his one rejection letter. "You let *that* discourage you? I don't believe you!" she gasped. "Let me read another one." Andrew dug out a second novel. "I like this one better than the first!" his new reader told him. "I really don't understand you. These should be published. What else have you got?" Before a month was up, Andrew's new friend had read all of Andrew's writing. "There's no reason any of this shouldn't be published" was her firm opinion. "Let me make submissions for you." Reluctant but curious, Andrew agreed, provided he himself was sheltered from the rejection process. Do I need to tell you that Andrew is now published, and hard at work on a new book?

Very often, it is our low self-worth, not our high standards, that keeps us from entering the fray. Like Andrew, we love our work and hate rejection. We hate it so much, we avoid the possibility of rejection. And when we do that, we avoid the possibility of acceptance as well.

In the winter, La Veta Pass is treacherous with ice. But travelers traverse it anyway, driving with great care. As creative travelers, we, too, can learn to traverse hostile conditions. We can make deals like Andrew did, and have a friend filter our creative lumps. Left to our own devices, many of us are shy—far too shy for our own creative good. It is for this reason that we need to enlist our friends as Believing Mirrors. We can learn to make the sandwich call, a call to a friend before doing something difficult, and a call to a friend afterward, saying, "I did it." It is part of our mythology about artists that artists are loners. This is not really true. What did the Impressionists paint? Lunch with one another. Artists have always needed encouragement, and wise artists learn to seek it out.

Fiona, an English actress, was making good strides in her London career but longed to come to America. Although she liked the stage, her true love was film, and Hollywood was where most movies were made. For two years Fiona dreamed of going to Hollywood. But she didn't actually do it. It was only when one of her theatrical directors assured her that he *knew* she could make it in film that Fiona gathered her courage and made the big leap across the Atlantic.

"Sometimes I think I'm a little crazy"—Fiona laughs—"being an English redhead in a world of bottle blondes, but most of the time I know that I've done the right thing. I'm just grateful I found the support that let me do it."

Sometimes the support that "lets us" do our art is external. More often, the support must be internal, a realization of our right to artistic actualization—the psychological fruit of Morning Pages, Artist Dates, and Walks.

ACHIEVING
ALTITUDE

Try this: Many times, we know a way we could advance our work, but we are too shy or frightened to try it. We hang back, waiting for that magic day when putting ourselves forward will be easier. As a producer remarked of staging musicals, "Whoever said it would be easy?" Take pen in hand and list five "next steps" you could take in support of your art. To do this, fill in the following phrase as rapidly as possible:

1. *A next step I could take for my art is*
   _____.

2. *A next step I could take for my art is*
   _____.

3. *A next step I could take for my art is*
   _____.

4. *A next step I could take for my art is*
   _____.

5. *A next step I could take for my art is*
   _____.

Being Festive

IT IS FIESTA WEEKEND in Taos. Traffic clogs the tiny streets. The ancient plaza overflows with tamales, tacos, and craft stands. Mariachi bands elbow out country-and-western and rock-and-roll. The sidewalks are thronged with tourists and locals. At midday, the police close the streets and the Fiesta parade unfurls itself. Float after float passes by with waving, dark-eyed Hispanic beauties. A troupe of Native American dancers prances past, fueled by two large tom-toms. Hundreds of horses dance skittishly, unnerved by the crowds and excitement. Pickup trucks are angled along the parade route, and observers clamber on their hoods and beds to get a better view. Fiesta is a visual spectacle: Colorful serapes cover hay wagons; cherub-cheeked children clutch piñatas and small American flags. It seems every business has a float, and every float has a cheering section. Young lovers, arms entwined, whisper to each other as cowboys and conquistadores clatter past. Like the tamales sold in the plaza, the parade is tasty.

Any sustained creative career requires a varied diet. As artists, we must seek out creative snacks. We must develop an appetite for a smorgasbord of creative fare. The parade, with its succulent tamales, might alternate with the cool sorbet of a chamber music ensemble. A traveling troupe of singing monks might offset a bout of children's theater. Art is an image-using system. Whenever we draw from our inner well, we must take care to restock it with new sights and sounds, new smells and tastes, new images for our artist to draw on.

Mitchell, a fine-arts photographer, lives in a loft in Chicago. His winter months are spent in urban surroundings, but every summer he takes to the road, camera in hand. The lonely reaches of Colorado, the well-polished boots and saddle gear of a cowboy, the deeply etched map of a Native American elder's face—these are the sights he trains his summer lens upon. A quarter century's experience as a photographer has taught Mitchell the importance of keeping a fresh eye. He doesn't want to go stale. His best work has an edgy originality, a newness no matter what the subject. His eye is kept fresh deliberately.

Emma, an arranger, credits a habit of road trips for giving her new musical ideas. "The more I look at, the better I arrange," she has remarked. And often, when she is stuck on a piece, she will get behind the wheel of the car for even a brief drive to town and come back with her musical ear refreshed.

Sights and sounds seem to help us no matter what our art form. Art is sensual, and when we consciously work to keep our senses alive, we are rewarded for our efforts with better art.

"As a novelist, I need a great deal of specificity," remarks Julian. "For writing to ring true, it must have sufficient detail. For me to write well, I must consciously refill my inner well of images. Driving, hiking, jogging—these things all help me. I have learned that what I put before my eyes comes straight out of my pen. When my eyes are stale, so is my writing."

Ours is a colorful world. It is filled with places and characters that can capture our imagination. The tiny Fiesta parade, winding its way to the town's ancient plaza, is just one such sight. Who would want to miss the golden palomino bobbing its snowy mane as it prances sideways up a small hill? Its rider wears a purple conquistador cape and a look of stern pride. A small black lamb and a larger gray one are ushered along the side of the street. They are the same size as the tiny burros pulling their gala flower-laden carts. During Fiesta, everyone is on holiday. Shopkeepers smile and loll in doorways. Tourists and natives alike stroll the streets. Music of many kinds fills the air from all directions. *"Aquí en Taos!"* someone shouts—Here in Taos.

BEING FESTIVE

Try this: The part of us that goes on Artist Dates might be called our inner explorer. It is an adventuresome part of the personality, daring to risk and to reach out. This part of us needs and deserves to be encouraged. Take pen in hand. Number from 1 to 10. Finish the following phrase as rapidly as possible:

1. *If it weren't too risky, I'd try*

   —————————————————.

2. *If it weren't too risky, I'd try*

   —————————————————.

3. *If it weren't too risky, I'd try*

   —————————————————.

4. *If it weren't too risky, I'd try*

   —————————————————.

5. *If it weren't too risky, I'd try*

   —————————————————.

6. *If it weren't too risky, I'd try*

    _____.

7. *If it weren't too risky, I'd try*

    _____.

8. *If it weren't too risky, I'd try*

    _____.

9. *If it weren't too risky, I'd try*

    _____.

10. *If it weren't too risky, I'd try*

    _____.

Seasons

LAST NIGHT IT SNOWED in Angel Fire. In Taos, the night was merely chilly—but autumn's coming. On the high ridges near the Ski Valley, the first aspen leaves are tinged with gold. The high mountain creeks are icy—even the Rio seems cold for a swim. Summers are brief in the high mountains. Autumn is long, golden, and glorious. We will not be staying for autumn this year. One of our musicals is being staged in New York, and it is time to pack the car for the long cross-country drive. This time we will take a southern route, looping through Texas, Oklahoma, and Missouri. The dogs are alert, eyeing the growing pile of luggage waiting to be taken to the car. They know this routine and are eager to get on with it. If they love Taos, with its river swims and expansive dog yard, they love New York, with its passing parade of fancy dogs and fancy owners. They will hunt pigeons again on Riverside Drive. The season has changed.

All creative lives have seasons, and we must learn to weather them. For me, the mountain summer has been a good season of writing—music in the mornings, prose in the afternoons. The autumn in New York will be a time of harvest. The seeds planted last year are bearing fruit. It seems to have taken forever, but the musical being staged, *The Medium at Large,* took only four years from its lightning strike of conception to its time on the stage. Four years is not very long in a creative life. I have been working at an opera now for five years, going on six. It will take at least two more years to complete it, although one of the great happinesses of the summer is that a finished first draft travels back with us to New York.

As artists, we must be in it for the long haul. We cannot measure ourselves by one season's success or failure. This year's novel may not see print for a decade. Last year's play may suddenly be called to the fore. It is a mistake to hook our work too closely to the mood of the market. Both the market and its mood will change. Work that is not in style at the moment will be in style again. We need patience.

Patience is not a trait that comes to most of us easily. Ours is a restless nature. This restlessness urges us to create. It is the first cause of books, plays, sonnets, and songs. But a career in the arts is a lot like marriage. It is worth learning patience for. It took me a decade to formulate the essays in my book *Walking in This World*. Sophy Burnham labored a decade on *The Treasure of Montségur*. For two years now, Natalie Goldberg has been at work on a nonfiction memoir of her spiritual life. My sister, a portrait artist, is finally overbooked with commissioned works—this after a scant twenty years in the studio.

Most overnight successes in the arts have nothing overnight about them—except for the fact that the sun of success now shines on them after a long, dark period of self-doubt. It has been said that all of success can be boiled down to two simple rules: the first, start something; the second, keep going. In Alcoholics Anonymous, there is a grim joke that the working definition of an alcoholic is "someone who drinks five minutes before the miracle." The point, of course, is to hang in, and the same advice might be given to artists.

A friend of mine, a sculptor, is in one of what he calls his "ugly-duckling periods." His work is changing, and its growth period is awkward. My friend has been sculpting for thirty years. He knows that growth is an ungainly process, and that sometimes we must do "bad" work to get to good work again. It is the same for me with writing: I will write along at a certain level, and then, one day, abruptly, my syntax will collapse. I'm in another growth period where nothing I write sounds quite right. Eventually, my style comes back together again, and up a notch—but that's eventually. My job, like all artists, is to hang in there while my syntax resembles pickup sticks.

They are predicting heavy snow for this winter. "They" are the mountain sages, elders who have lived here a long time and experienced seasons of drought and rain. The extra moisture would be good for the valley. The drought burned the needles on many evergreen trees. Good snow would restore them to health. In the long view, it all balances out. But that is in the long view. It is our job to find it.

SEASONS

Try this: Most of us are adept at seeing what we fail to do. We are not so accomplished, or accustomed, to counting what has been done. And yet, self-worth can be built upon a bedrock of creative actions well taken. Take pen in hand. This is your creative résumé. Set aside one hour and take pen to page, going back to the beginning of your life and listing any and all creative accomplishments. This tool, used by Arts Anonymous, a 12-step program for artists, is very powerful.

Epilogue

I AM BACK IN NEW YORK. The return drive cross-country was uneventful, but the entry into New York was an adventure. I changed apartments, from my Riverside Drive perch to one with city views. My writing desk now looks out across brownstones, down avenues where passersby duck their heads under shiny black umbrellas while a cold late-autumn rain stings their skin. The leaves have turned and the season is turning. On my morning walks, a light mist rises from the reservoir in Central Park. The maple leaves underfoot are lightly frosted. Tiny plumes of steamy breath puff up from my cocker spaniel's muzzle. It is good to be back. It is my hope that you have enjoyed your time spent with this small book. Creativity is an ongoing process. We can always become both larger and stronger. It is my hope that you will consider yourself on an open-ended adventure. I think of myself as a companion on the trail.

Julia Cameron has been an active artist for more than thirty years. She is the author of nineteen books, fiction and nonfiction, including *The Artist's Way, Walking in This World, The Vein of Gold,* and *The Right to Write,* her bestselling works on the creative process. A novelist, playwright, songwriter, and poet, Cameron divides her time between Manhattan and the high deserts of New Mexico.

To order call 1-800-788-6262 or send your order to:

Penguin Group (USA) Inc.
P.O. Box 12289 Dept. B
Newark, NJ 07101-5289

Walking in This World	1-58542-261-4 paper	$15.95
	1-58542-183-9 hardcover	$24.95
The Artist's Way Tenth Anniversary Edition	1-58542-146-4 paper	$15.95
The Artist's Way Tenth Anniversary Gift Edition	1-58542-147-2 hardcover	$40.00
The Artist's Way Audio	0-87477-852-2	$18.95
The Right to Write	0-58542-009-3 paper	$12.95
	0-87447-937-6 hardcover	$19.95
The Vein of Gold	0-87477-879-4 paper	$15.95
	0-87477-836-0 hardcover	$23.95
God Is No Laughing Matter	1-58542-128-6 paper	$13.95
	1-58542-065-4 hardcover	$19.95
The Artist's Date Book	0-87477-653-8	$14.95
The Artist's Way Morning Pages Journal	0-87477-886-7 paper	$14.95
Heart Steps	0-87477-899-9 paper	$9.95
	0-87477-901-4 audio	$10.95
Blessings	0-87477-906-5 paper	$9.95
	0-87477-907-3 audio	$11.95
Transitions	0-87477-995-2 paper	$9.95
	0-87477-996-0 audio	$11.95
Inspirations: Meditations from The Artist's Way	1-58542-102-2 paper	$6.95
The Writer's Life: Insights from		
The Right to Write	1-58542-103-0 paper	$6.95
Supplies: A Pilot's Manual for Creative Flight	1-58542-066-2 paper	$14.95
God Is Dog Spelled Backwards	1-58542-062-X paper	$9.95